A Concise Guide to the
PARISH
CHURCH

A Concise Guide to the

PARISH
CHURCH

RICHARD HAYMAN

TEMPUS

First published 2007

Tempus Publishing Limited
The Mill, Brimscombe Port,
Stroud, Gloucestershire, GL5 2QG
www.tempus-publishing.com

ISBN 978 0 7524 4095 8

Typesetting and origination by Tempus Publishing Limited
Printed in Great Britain

CONTENTS

1
INTRODUCTION

Churches embody more of our history than any other type of building. Better still, they are open to the public – or ought to be – and, because the vast majority of them continue in use, they have not been sanitised or spruced up for presentation to the visitor in a controlled setting. Churches are museums for the independent of mind. Unlike history, which we tend to look at in a single point in time, a building presents us with a long timespan in a single view. No building is ever fixed in a single moment. This is especially true of churches, which in over 1500 years of Christian history have endured a remarkable number of changes while continuing to perform the same specific function (1). Often it is the blend of these time periods that holds the attention, and the manner in which a building can remain artistically convincing when it has work of many different periods. It certainly makes churches an inexhaustible subject of interest.

The purpose of this book is to explain why churches look like they do. Churches were created to serve particular needs and consequently their form is determined by their function. The church was conceived as the setting for the practice of the Christian observances and, in the vast majority of cases, was adapted when those observances were altered. But church architecture also had a symbolic function. It expressed ideas about the doctrine of Christianity, expressed something of the social status and cultural sophistication of its patrons, and was often constrained by technical or economic realities. A medieval church was conceived as an earthly embodiment of the heavenly Jerusalem, and its architecture, decoration and liturgy all reflected that aim. It is what the Victorians tried to revive. Norman and Gothic architectural styles were developed to express this religious devotion and, especially before the Reformation,

1 The Anglo-Saxon carving of Christ with his hand raised in blessing was discovered in 1931 at Barnack (Huntingdonshire). It is an enduring symbol that links us with over a thousand years of our history and art history

the splendour of the church reinforced the centrality of religion in people's lives. What is less well-appreciated is the degree to which church architecture was directly the work of the local communities themselves, being an expression of popular religion and popular culture. A period of nearly 300 years following the Reformation produced churches and a liturgy with less heavenly aspirations and a more worldly appearance. The manner in which new requirements were incorporated into older buildings has ensured that churches bear the grain of English and Welsh history within them.

2
CHURCH AND COMMUNITY

Before describing the form of the first churches, some space must be given over to the development of Christianity in Britain and to the evolution of what became the parish system. Christianity reached Roman Britain in the fourth century, although the extent of the faith and the exact nature of religious practices are not well understood. The faith survived, in fact it seems to have flourished, after the demise of Roman administration, except in the south-eastern parts of Britain where the dominant incomers – Angles, Saxons and Jutes – were pagan. Despite the independence of Celtic Christianity, the prevailing system of parish and cathedral churches belongs to the orthodox Christianity of Rome. Its influence on Britain began when Pope Gregory I sent Augustine, abbot of a monastery in Rome, to Britain in 597 on a mission to preach the new faith among the heathen English.

Conversion was first achieved with the social elites, whether or not they accepted Christianity by conviction or expediency, and henceforth it was disseminated from the top level of society downwards. The first churches to be founded in Anglo-Saxon England were monasteries and minsters. Monasteries were communities of men or women devoted to a life of prayer and contemplation. They probably existed in Roman Britain, and they existed in Ireland by the fifth century and in Wales by the sixth century. In England, monasteries followed the Rule of St Benedict, written in the early sixth century, which became the foundation of Roman monasticism. It involved a community devoted to prayer in a structured daily liturgy, reading of sacred texts, and manual work. Foundation of a monastery and an endowment of land for its subsistence was an act of piety on the part of the elite, and a form that was to flourish in the twelfth and thirteenth centuries.

'Minster' is derived from the Old English form of the Latin *monaste-rium* and included houses of secular priests (priests who had not taken a vow of obedience to a monastic Rule) as well as of monks. Minsters and their priests served the needs of the secular community and were distributed according to land ownership or administrative districts. By the tenth century tithes were payable to the minsters, giving them some resemblance to parish churches, but they served a much greater geographical area than later churches. In addition, private churches were built by landowners as an expression of their piety and their social status. By the eleventh century there were four categories of church serving the lay population: head minsters (cathedrals), lesser minsters, estate churches with graveyards and field churches without graveyards. As the lesser minsters gradually lost their pre-eminence, and the estate and field churches gained independent parochial status, the local parish system of churches evolved in the eleventh and twelfth centuries on a much older pattern of church building.

In Wales the establishment of Christianity took a different course. Myths about the early Celtic Church abound, but it is certain that the development of Christianity in Wales owed much to the key saints: Dyfrig in the fifth century, and Illtud and David in the sixth century. Illtud founded the monastery at Llantwit Major, from which emerged other important early Christian figures such as St Samson, Paul Aurelian and the historian Gildas. David belonged to a tradition of ascetic monasticism in Wales that characterised the Celtic church. The traditional Celtic monastery, or *clas*, often later became a parish church. So did the *llan*, the consecrated enclosures in which Christians buried their dead and with which many of the Celtic saints – Padarn, Teilo, Catwg, Gwynno – are associated. Churches were built on these sites long after they became consecrated ground.

The long independence of Christianity in Wales was one factor in its resistance to the international embrace of the Roman Church. For example, Wales did not accept the date of Roman Easter until 768. Nevertheless, differences between Celtic and Roman Christianity have often been exaggerated. Norman political conquest of Wales was followed by the regularisation of its church, but it had more to do with administration than theology. Wales hitherto had no Benedictine monasteries, its dioceses were indeterminate and most of its churches were built of timber, a situation that was only slowly rectified. Norman architecture is much less common in Wales than it is in England.

MEDIEVAL LITURGY

The parish church liturgy in the Middle Ages was based on the Sunday
services of Matins, Mass and Evensong, of which the Mass was the best
attended. The basic division within the church was the sacred section,
i.e. the chancel where the priests conducted the services, and the secular
section, i.e. the nave and its aisles for the lay worshippers. There were no seats
in the nave, requiring the congregation to stand or, occasionally, to kneel.
The congregation had no active role in the Mass, which was a ceremony

Above, left and right: 2, 3 A series of sixteenth-century bench ends at Trull (Somerset)
depicts a religious procession. At the head of the procession is a crucifer and behind
it is a priest carrying a reliquary with holy relics

conducted on their behalf by the priests. For this reason the Mass, especially the less important parts of the ceremony, was often a meeting point
during which parish business was discussed. The most significant part
of the Mass was signalled by the Elevation of the Host, at which point
the bread and wine were consecrated and became the body and blood
of Christ. This was the doctrine of transubstantiation that had been
established at the Lateran council of 1215. The lay worshippers took the
sacrament normally once a year, at Easter. Mass was expected to be said
every day of the week, although the laity were not expected to attend,
except for the special Masses associated with holy days, for example those
dedicated to the patron saint of the church. Special occasions were also
attended by processions, for example in the display of holy relics (2, 3).

Preaching only became common in parish churches from the fourteenth century, under the influence of the newer mendicant orders
of friars. Unlike cloistered monks, friars lived according to a Rule
but dedicated themselves to working and preaching among the lay
community. Their influence encouraged parish priests to take up preaching themselves, and to teach their congregation the elements of the faith
– the Apostles' Creed, the Lord's Prayer and the Ten Commandments.
Sermons were delivered in English and normally in the form of an allegorical tale, or *exemplum*, in which a story was used to convey a moral
message (4). Until the fifteenth century, when pulpits begin to appear
in parish churches, these were probably not delivered from any special
fixture, and nor were they a regular part of worship.

In addition to its regular services, occasional offices of the church
brought a religious context to every phase of life. There were seven sacraments in the medieval church, of which all but the ordination of priests
directly involved the parish community. The other sacraments were baptism, confirmation, Mass, marriage, penance (or confession) and extreme
unction. Baptism admitted infants to the Christian community which
was essential for salvation. As Langland put it in *Piers the Ploughman*,
'except a man be born of water and of the spirit, he cannot enter the
Kingdom of Heaven'. Confirmation was the rite of passage whereby
children were admitted as adult Christians and were able to receive the
sacrament at Easter. Marriage was both a sacrament and a legal contract. Among wealthier people, a legal contract was agreed in a secular
ceremony known as a 'troth-plight'. The marriage ceremony took place
in the porch, after which the bridal party was taken into the church to

4 A bench end at Lakenheath (Suffolk) brings to life one of the sermons preached by the friars, warning of the tricks played by the devil to steal the souls of the righteous. The carving on the armrest depicts a tigress fooled into looking into a mirror where she thinks she can see her cubs, allowing a hunter to escape with the real cubs

celebrate a nuptial Mass. In preparation for communion at Easter the priest heard the confessions of his parishioners, which covered matters such as sins done to other people and deficiencies in spiritual knowledge.

Death and the preparation for it took the parish priests away from the church building. They were expected to visit the sick and to anoint the dying in a ceremony known as extreme unction. The tolling of the church bell announced that a funeral was to be conducted, which was accompanied by a requiem mass. The following Sunday at Mass the names of the dead were read out and prayers were solicited for their souls. Praying for the souls of the departed bound together the living and the dead and helped to cement the community. Everybody would one day need the prayers of fellow parishioners.

Commemorative prayers and Masses were organised through chantries and guilds. The rich built chantry chapels or founded colleges of priests, an act that was intended to ensure their future spiritual welfare, as well as being a pious use of disposable income, an expression of social status and a hope that the social order would be maintained in the next life. A collegiate church was one where a patron endowed a college of secular priests to celebrate Mass and the offices of the church. A chantry was an endowment that paid for a priest to offer prayers and say masses for the soul of its founder, usually in perpetuity. Sometimes the chapel occupied the east end of an aisle, or they could be in separate chapels, in which might be the founders' tomb. Chantry chapels became popular from the fourteenth century – St Mary Redcliffe in Bristol had 24 chantry priests by 1380. Guilds performed the same (and other) functions as chantries, serving their subscribing members on a collective basis. Like chantries, guilds also had their own altars for the saying of commemorative masses. Members of guilds tended to share either a locality or a common trade. At Ludlow (Shropshire) the principal guild was the Palmers' (i.e. pilgrims') Guild, founded c.1250. By 1284 donations and subscriptions paid for the subsistence of three priests, but by the fifteenth century there were up to ten. The clergymen lived in a college and sang the daily offices of the church.

5 One of the finest medieval wooden chests is at Malpas (Cheshire), a thirteenth-century work reinforced by ironwork of very high quality

Certain aspects of the medieval liturgy were funded by the parish community. Among the responsibilities placed upon the parish were the requirement to provide the correct vestments, books and utensils, which were stored in wooden chests. A few of them have survived. Malpas (Cheshire) has a wooden chest strengthened by fine die-stamped wrought-iron straps (5). Other notable examples have relief carving, as at Crediton (Devon), Dersingham (Norfolk) and Faversham (Kent).

CHURCH BUILDING AND THE COMMUNITY

In the twelfth and thirteenth centuries patronage of churches was the privilege of major landholders such as local lords, religious institutions and senior church officials. It was they who appointed the priests. By the fifteenth century patronage was far more diverse as communities and wealthy tradesmen began to take control of church building and decoration. Although the wealthy were the most conspicuous benefactors of churches, all of the lay community were able to participate in the building and adornment of the church. Small donations contributed to everything from altar frontals to Somerset towers. Rebuilding and adornment of churches by their parishioners expresses the vitality of parish life and the importance of the communal identity in late medieval Britain. Nevertheless, responsibility for the church building was divided. Patrons were still responsible for the chancel, while the parishioners were responsible for the remainder of the building. There are several cases where the chancel of a parish church was used by monks as the outlying cell of the larger monastery. They include some fine parish churches like Dunster (Somerset), Wymondham (Norfolk) and Bromfield (Shropshire).

The great age of popular piety was the late fifteenth and sixteenth centuries, when church building (or rebuilding) and furnishing was undertaken on an unprecedented scale. Even so, ambitious buildings were expensive operations and relied upon a steady cash flow, which was often difficult to sustain. The consequence was that building projects became prolonged or even unfinished. The tower at East Bergholt (Suffolk) was never finished. Nor was the tower of Ruishton (Somerset), which has no crown. Wealthy individuals often led the way with ambitious new building projects. There are several notable examples in Gloucestershire, like Chipping Camden, extended from the 1450s, led by the wealthy clothier William Bradway (6). Northleach was also rebuilt from the 1450s, under the initiative of John Fortey, who gave £300 to the

6 Chipping Camden (Gloucestershire) was one of the centres of the wool and cloth trades of Gloucestershire. Its parish church, with a fine tower, expresses both popular piety and secular prosperity

building of the nave in 1458. Such churches are often misleadingly called wool churches at a time and in places where the economy was never so dependent upon a single resource. The Lincolnshire Wolds was prosperous sheep country in the later medieval period but saw little great church rebuilding. South-west England always had a more diverse, mixed farming economy and in the case of Somerset and Devon, a long history of prosperity and a rich heritage of late medieval churches.

Individual donations to Church building included money left in wills, many of which specified particular building schemes. The other main source of income was the special fundraising events organised by the churchwardens. Churches and churchyards were used for markets, fairs and church ales. Communal gatherings, including May and Whitsun festivals, were organised by the parish and in the late Middle Ages became an important source of revenue for building and furnishing the church. By the mid-thirteenth century the church hierarchy disapproved of holding such events inside the building but the churchyard continued to be one of the few public spaces in the community. At Eltham (London) use of the church for secular gatherings continued until 1511.

THE REFORMATION

The Reformation had a profound effect on parish churches. It was the result of a long campaign for liturgical reform, and was precipitated by political events. The first act of the Reformation occurred when the Act of Supremacy was passed in 1534. It made Henry VIII head of the Church and removed the Pope from power over English affairs. Monasticism had been in long-term decline, but the abbeys and priories remained powerful and often wealthy institutions that also had allegiances abroad. They were all dissolved between 1536 and 1539 and their landholdings passed to the crown. Some of the monastic churches, or parts of them, became parish churches, the origin of many grand town churches like those at Pershore (Worcestershire), Sherborne (Dorset), Tewkesbury (Gloucestershire) and Malmesbury (Wiltshire). In most cases, however, the church was not wanted and quickly fell into decay, also acting as an easy quarry for building materials. It was the landholdings of the monasteries that were important, many of which would later be the basis of the country estates of the aristocracy.

Religious reform came with these institutional changes. The Reformation was also a profound cultural revolution. Concern about excessive and superstitious ritual saw the removal of much of the religious art in churches. To a certain extent the Reformation can be seen as the substitution of the word for the image. And the word was no longer Latin. In 1536 Thomas Cromwell issued the Ten Articles and Injunctions, which required priests to conduct services in English, and for a copy of an English Bible to be placed in every church. One unintended consequence was the flourishing of native languages – in less than a century English had produced two of its supreme works, the King James Bible, known as the Authorised Version, and the works of Shakespeare. The first complete Welsh Bible, translated by William Salesbury and William Morgan, was published in 1588, the beginning of a long religious literary tradition. Although it would be exaggeration to claim that the Bible saved the Welsh language, the absence of a Cornish Bible probably contributed to the decline of that native language.

The radical changes to parish churches also began with the Ten Articles and Injunctions. It placed the first limitations upon images within the church, and specifically identified some as idolatrous. Among Protestant criticisms of traditional religion was abhorrence of the practice of praying for the intercession of saints on the part of the lay people. Images or statues were the focus of these prayers, or cults, and many were therefore removed from the church. The pace of change was stepped up after the accession of Edward VI in 1547. All images were either removed from the church, or painted representations were whitewashed over or defaced. It amounted to the most intense episode of iconoclasm ever inflicted on the Church. In some churches there is visible evidence for this, like the defaced saints on the rood screen at Southwold (Suffolk) and the images painted over and replaced with Biblical texts at Binham Priory (Norfolk) (7).

Protestant reformers did not believe in purgatory and so in the Chantries Act of 1547 commemorative masses were abolished, rendering chantry and guild altars obsolete. The *Book of Common Prayer*, first published in 1549 but revised in 1552, set out the new form of worship to be used in the Church of England (a Welsh edition was published in 1551). The sacraments were either stripped of much of their mystical and visual appurtenances or, like penance and extreme unction, were abolished entirely. Protestants did not believe in transubstantiation, that the

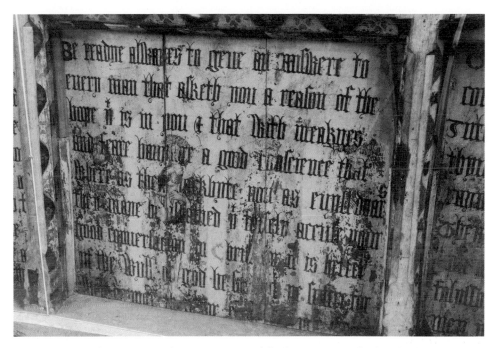

7 At the Reformation, Binham Priory (Norfolk) became a parish church. The painted images of saints on the rood screen were whitened out and replaced by Biblical texts in English. Substitution of word for image sums up much of what the Reformation was about

bread and wine turned into the body and blood of Christ once it had been consecrated. The Eucharist henceforth became a simpler symbolic commemoration of the Last Supper. It was de-mystified by removing stone altars and replacing them with wooden communion tables, whilst the chancel was opened up to admit the congregation.

THE POST-REFORMATION CHURCH

Although there was a brief reversion to Catholicism under Queen Mary (1553-58), the new Anglican Church prevailed under Elizabeth I (1558-1603). The Thirty-Nine Articles issued in 1563 made a definitive statement of Christian doctrine which all priests and people were obliged to obey. Those that did not or could not formed Puritan sects, or clung to their Catholic doctrine, both illegal at this time.

Political upheavals of the seventeenth century had a major impact on the Church. In 1631 Charles I appointed William Laud Archbishop of Canterbury, under whose direction church ritual moved in a decidedly Catholic direction. Under the Commonwealth the pendulum swung back in favour of radical Puritans and there was a further wave of iconoclasm in English churches. During the Commonwealth the Prayer Book had been replaced by *The Directory of Public Worship*, but a new authorised version of the *Book of Common Prayer* was issued in 1662, which was still widely used in the twentieth century. In the seventeenth and eighteenth centuries the sermon became more important than the Eucharist, except for a short interlude in the 1630s. Less emphasis on the sacramental aspects of Christianity had many effects, including the adoption of the secular instead of a sacred language, plainer vestments, and less decorated interiors, where visual symbolism and allegory thrived principally on funeral monuments, and on the Royal Arms that signified the head of the Church (*8*).

8 At Weston-under-Lizard (Staffordshire) the iron altar rails are adorned with a flamboyant Royal Arms of Queen Anne. After the Restoration of 1660 all parish churches were required to display the arms of the head of the Church of England

After the Reformation church building was never again to be the community project that it was in the late Middle Ages, although the tradition has lived on in the furnishing of the church and in its restoration campaigns. By contrast, labouring and mercantile classes increasingly left the Established Church to found their own nonconformist denominations. The earliest of these, such as the Baptists, Society of Friends (or Quakers), Congregationalists (known as Independents or *Annibynwyr* in Welsh-speaking communities) and Unitarians were formed before the 1689 Toleration Act allowed them to meet freely and build their own chapels. The great monuments to popular religion were henceforth the nonconformist chapels.

In the eighteenth century parish church patronage was largely in the hands of the gentry and aristocracy, while the clergy were also drawn substantially from those ranks of society. Pew rents ensured that the social hierarchy was maintained inside the church. One of its consequences was the growth of non-conformism, especially in places like the North of England and in Wales where the established church was weak. The Anglican church was slow to cater for the demands of industrial settlements and expanding cities where the provision for churchgoing was difficult or non-existent. It was saved by government intervention.

In 1818 Parliament passed the Church Building Act that established a Commission to oversee the erection of new churches in newly populated districts, with the help of a grant of £1 million. Over the next decade and a half 97 state-funded churches were built, most of which were in London and the industrial conurbations of the Midlands and the North. Parliament approved a second grant in 1824 which contributed a portion of the funds required for a new building, the remainder being raised locally (9). When the work of the Church Building Commission ceased in 1856 over 600 new parish churches had been built, the majority of them in urban locations. Nevertheless, a great shock awaited the political and social Establishment. A religious census taken in 1851 indicated that only 52 per cent of the population attended church on Easter Sunday of that year. It proved to be a wake-up call. The great building and restoration of the nation's churches took place after that date, but without the subsidies that had propped up the Church in the early part of the century.

9 Glyntaf (Glamorgan) was built in 1838 by T.H. Wyatt and was designed to seat 800 people. It received a parliamentary grant of £414 towards its £2500 total cost. The remainder was mainly provided by the Lenox and Crawshay families, local industrialists

Interest in the medieval liturgy was revived in the nineteenth century. A group of Oxford clergymen issued a series of pamphlets between 1833 and 1841 under the general heading *Tracts for the Times*, which advocated a return to Catholic doctrine and a re-emphasis on the sacraments. Known as the Oxford Movement, or Tractarians, they were in sympathy with a pressure group known as the Cambridge Camden Society. This was an architectural society that advocated the study of medieval art and architecture *and* that restoration of old churches and building of new ones should follow medieval principles and practice. It advanced its ideas through a journal, *The Ecclesiologist*, first published in 1841 and from whence it took its later name, the Ecclesiological Society. However, some aspects of the Protestant centuries remained in favour, such as congregational hymn singing. The English language was also retained, but its preference for the by now archaic English of the 1662 Prayer Book and 1611 Bible went some way to reviving the old notion of a secular and a sacred language. Inspired by medieval architecture and by accounts of medieval religious practices, the Eucharist was reinstated at the heart of Christian practice. The new interest in decoration to dignify, mystify and create a visual spectacle of the liturgy extended from architecture to the revival of applied arts like stained glass and to priests' vestments.

The private sector paid for the majority of nineteenth-century churches, whether in town or country. In London it was so successful that church building exceeded demand, with a result that churches in the capital have been in retreat for a century. In the countryside the church remained a symbol of local power and social responsibility, although many of its most notable Victorian churches – like Skelton (Yorkshire), Hoar Cross (Staffordshire) and Highnam (Gloucestershire) – were commemorative in inspiration and stand as monuments to their benefactors.

The legacy of the Anglican revival is still with us, although from the second half of the twentieth century there has been a relaxation in the solemnity of church services, with some parishes more 'low church' than others. The twentieth century saw a decline in church attendance and in 1920 the disestablishment of the Church in Wales. Declining attendance is the biggest challenge faced by the Church. It has led to increasing closures of rural and urban churches, an alarming trend that was partly alleviated by the foundation in 1969 by the Redundant Churches Fund. Now known as the Churches Conservation Trust, it looks after an increasing number of churches in England no longer in use for regular worship. The developing sophistication of conservation techniques has increased the cost of maintaining and restoring churches, further adding to the burden on parish communities. Some vicars would gladly move out of their old churches, disdaining them as uneconomical and no longer fit for purpose. On the contrary, only by remaining in its churches, some of which have been the site of worship for over a 1000 years, will the church stand where it belongs, at the core of the nation's heritage.

3

THE PLACE

It is always worth looking beyond the boundaries of the churchyard for clues as to why churches were built in particular places. Often the location of a church can only be explained by factors that are no longer apparent. Many churches stand isolated in farmland, giving no clue to the former settlements they served, like Stocklinch Ottersey (Somerset) or Birkby (North Yorkshire) (*colour plate 1*). Low Ham (Somerset) was built in 1629 and stands in a farmyard, with no sign of the long-demolished mansion house that stood close by and was the reason the church was built. In other places, like Honeychurch (Devon) or Shocklach (Cheshire) you might wonder if there has ever been a congregation to serve.

Numerous considerations account for the site of medieval churches. In some places, especially in Celtic Britain, a parish church began as a monastery, or *clas*, perhaps associated with the birthplace or life of a saint. Penally (Pembrokeshire) was the birthplace of St Teilo and was an important early Christian site. The present church is thirteenth-century in origin but evidence of the earlier monastery is confined to fragments of four crosses, including a large tenth-century wheel-headed cross. Likewise Llantwit Major, near Cardiff, was founded as a monastery by St Illtud *c.*500. The earliest parts of the present church date back only as far as the twelfth century, but it retains Celtic crosses of the ninth and tenth centuries (*10*).

ASSOCIATION WITH PRE-CHRISTIAN SITES

In a few cases parish churches can be seen to have been built on pre-Christian sites, although far fewer than is commonly supposed.

10 A monastery was founded at Llantwit Major (Glamorgan) by St Illtyd *c*.500.
Although the present building dates only from the twelfth century its ninth-century
crosses indicate a much earlier origin. On the right is the Houelt Stone, which
has an inscription explaining that the stone was prepared by Houelt for the soul
of his father Res, possibly Hywel ap Rhys (died 886). On the left is the Samson
stone, of which only the shaft has survived, and whose inscription survives only in
fragmentary form

The well-known examples are well known because they are exceptional. Rudston (East Riding) has a prehistoric standing stone in its churchyard, and stands at the convergence of three linear contemporary earthworks known as cursus monuments (*11*). Already more then 2000 years old when the church was built, Rudston church is unlikely to represent direct continuity between the Bronze Age and Christianity. If the stone or the site was venerated as a special place in the pagan post-Roman period, it was surely for different reasons from those for which it was built. Likewise Knowlton (Dorset), a now ruined church, was built inside a Neolithic henge monument. Conversely, at Avebury (Wiltshire) and Stanton Drew (Somerset) the church was built close to but outside of the stone circles.

Roman sites are associated with medieval churches for a number of possible reasons, although continuity of the Christian faith from the fourth century does not appear to be one of them. Roman buildings provided dressed masonry and places where building stone or bricks can be seen re-used in churches are described in the next chapter. Roman places may have remained centres of political power, if only in a symbolic sense, and in such cases building a church there would be

11 Rudston church (East Riding) is sited close to a Bronze Age standing stone. The stone is at the convergence of contemporary linear earthworks known as cursus monuments after the famous example at Stonehenge

logical. Churches associated with Roman towns and forts or fortresses include St John at Chester, Llaneblig near Caernarfon (Gwynedd) and Godmanchester (Huntingdonshire). Churches built on Roman temples or mausoleums, or near Roman and post-Roman cemeteries, all of which may have been cult centres in the pagan post-Roman period, show continuity between pagan and Christian faith. Examples are at Lullingstone (Kent), Northover near Ilchester Roman town (Somerset), and St Mary de Lode in Gloucester, the exterior of which looks almost entirely nineteenth-century.

Wells are a group of cult centres closely associated with churches, from the grand – at Bath and Wells – to the humble, such as the ruined Capel Bigawdin (Carmarthenshire), which has a stream running beneath it. Well is a misleading term for a sacred site that usually refers to a spring, from which water is collected in a basin. The Welsh *ffynnon* is much better in this respect. The symbolic and magical potential of running water emerging from the earth is not exclusive to pagan views of the world. In Christianity, spiritual rebirth through baptism is an essential rite of passage. The existence of wells certainly influenced the siting of churches, although they are not always visible, as on the reclaimed marshes at Tywyn (Gwynedd), or at Barton-upon-Humber (Lincolnshire) where the wells were enveloped by enlargement of the church in the thirteenth century. In many cases wells had curative properties, but the parish church was built near it rather than incorporating the well into the consecrated ground of the churchyard. Cornwall has numerous examples – Sancreed, Altarnun and St Levan. Chapels at holy wells are mainly not of parochial status, such as St Winifred's Chapel at Holywell (Flintshire) and Clether and St Cleer (Cornwall).

Hilltop churches are a phenomenon in parts of England and are usually dedicated to St Michael or St Catherine. In many of the dramatic examples, like the churches at St Michael's Mount and Roche (both Cornwall), Abbotsbury (Dorset) and Glastonbury Tor (Somerset), they were not parish churches. Brentor (Devon) is one exception to this rule. On Burrow Mump, once an island amid saltwater and freshwater marshes until they were drained to form the Somerset Levels, was a private chapel that only became a parish church after the Reformation. More stark and surreal than its famous neighbour at Glastonbury Tor, Burrow Mump was a particularly impractical place for Sunday worship, weddings and funerals – the old and inform stood more chance of reaching the top in a coffin than they would under their own steam. The old church was replaced in 1829 by a new, anonymous church at the foot of the hill. The ruined church on the hill is now among the most romantic of Christian monuments.

The origin of such isolated churches was the desire to establish the religious life in places remote from society, the equivalent of the Biblical desert. Some hilltop churches, like Breedon-on-the-Hill (Leicestershire) and Minster-in-Sheppey (Kent) were originally monastic sites. The coastal equivalent of the hilltop was the promontory or peninsula, which provided the same sense of self-containment and isolation. The church on Holy Island (Northumberland) stands next to the former monastery of Lindisfarne. Llangwyfan, just off the west coast of Anglesey, has only the waves for company and looks more like a site for a monastery than a parish church.

RURAL CHURCHES

Most churches were built where people lived. If the church is now isolated then it is a sign that the settlement has shifted over time, or shrank or has been abandoned. Proximity to the centre of local power is also a common factor determining the site of a rural parish church. In the Marches there are many twelfth-century churches built close to fortified houses, usually now identified by the motte and bailey, of which Kilpeck and Eardisley (Herefordshire) are notable examples. In the case of Kilpeck the accompanying village was later abandoned, leaving the church alone next to a farm. In the English Midlands, Anglo-Saxon churches with towers are associated with earthwork enclosures at Barton-upon-Humber (Lincolnshire) and Earls Barton (Northamptonshire). In most cases there is no trace of the corresponding house but it has been argued that churches tend to occupy high ground because they were originally established next to the halls of local lords, for which a high vantage point was the preferred location. One of the unintended consequences of estate origin is that such churches are not always logically spaced. Occasionally parish churches that originated as estate churches are found next to each other. Among Norfolk villages Reepham, South Walsham and Antingham each have two adjoining churches.

It was not only early churches that stood next to the seat of local power. Countless medieval churches stand next to former manor houses, although in the vast majority of cases the houses have been rebuilt and appear much later than the church. In places like Pitchford (Shropshire) and Brympton D'Evercy (Somerset) the church stands in private gardens of a great house. In other cases the former manorial centre has declined in status and is now a farm. There are numerous small farmyard churches, like those of Toller Fratrum (Dorset), Swell (Somerset) and Southrop (Gloucestershire).

The conjunction of mansion and church continued after the Reformation, when the aristocratic estates began to flourish. The architecture of these churches needed to harmonise with the main house. Staunton Harold (Leicestershire) church was built in 1653-65 next to Staunton Harold Hall, in a Gothic revival style that sat comfortably with the Jacobean style of the house as it then was. Church and house were still built close together in the eighteenth century, as at Great Witley (Worcestershire) of c.1720 and Gunton Hall (Norfolk) of 1765-9. However the eighteenth century was the age of the landscape park, in which a church was a fully integrated component of the conceit. Sometimes the church was a medieval establishment, like at Fawsley (Northamptonshire), where the village was removed when the park was created, leaving the church an isolated building visible from the mansion of the Knightley family. Orchardleigh (Somerset) shows the survival of this trend to the nineteenth century. At Shobdon (Herefordshire) a new church was built in 1752 to suit the design of a landscape park, at which time the old Norman church was demolished, leaving only its decorated doorways as landscape features. A similar case is Croome d'Abitot (Worcestershire), where a new church was built in 1763 by Capability Brown and Robert Adam as an integral component of Brown's landscape park.

The nineteenth century saw no let up in country-house building and the desire to build churches almost as private chapels. In many cases, like Studley Royal (North Yorkshire) of 1870-8 and Clumber Park (Nottinghamshire) of 1886-9, they are among the most lavish churches of the period and their grandeur has made them personal memorials. Nineteenth-century landowners also built churches in their estate villages.

URBAN CHURCHES

Different considerations applied to the foundation and site of urban churches. By the end of the eleventh century English towns were well-endowed with churches – Norwich had 46 churches and chapels in 1086, Exeter 29, and the *Life of Thomas Becket* composed in the 1170s boasts 126 parish churches in London. Many of these churches were built by individuals or groups of citizens with neighbourhood or other collective interests. The *Anglo-Saxon Chronicle* records that the church of St Olave in York was founded by Earl Siward, who was buried there in 1055. Association with individuals or trade is sometimes commemorated in the idiosyncratic naming of urban churches. London has many of them, like St Mary Woolnoth (Wulfnoth), St Clement Danes, and St Clement Eastcheap (from 'ceap' meaning market). Not all private churches acquired parish status as some of them ceased to function and were converted to other uses. The number of churches in a town fluctuated with its changing fortunes. Norwich had 57 churches in 1254, 48 by the mid-fourteenth century and 35 by the mid-fifteenth century. Today 35 churches remain standing, although only 11 remain in use.

In towns like Winchester and Exeter the parish churches were built on the main thoroughfares or, probably because of limited space, in the back yards of buildings on the main thoroughfares. Having to follow the alignment of street plans meant that it was difficult for all churches to face east, or even the point of sunrise on the day of the church's patron saint (whether that was the strict norm of medieval parish churches is not certain). Lack of space inhibited the provision of large graveyards, for which reason many town churches rub shoulders with neighbouring secular buildings, quite different from the setting of rural parish churches. At Winchester the cathedral served as the town graveyard until the fourteenth century, while at Chichester the dead were buried either in the cathedral cemetery or a cemetery outside the town walls known as The Litten. Where churches were lucky enough to have graveyards, they were often also used as markets until official disapproval moved them out of the churchyard during the thirteenth century. Haphazard development created irregular urban parish boundaries, and resulted in the close proximity of many parish churches, which remains a feature of historic towns in England – such as Saints Alkmund and Julian in the centre of Shrewsbury (Shropshire).

Corner sites between major and minor streets were much favoured because they allowed the church to be a prominent building without occupying the major intersections where trade was focused. Stamford St George (Lincolnshire) and St Martin in Micklegate, York, preserve this position. Another favoured position for medieval urban churches was beside, or above, a gateway. All the major towns and cities had or have them – London, Chester, York, Canterbury, Winchester and Exeter. Bristol had churches at its south and east gates, and two churches at its north gate, of which only St John the Baptist remains standing, with passageway beneath it (*12*). Warwick has a similar arrangement of first-floor chapels over its East and West Gates. Gateways had a spiritual resonance as a threshold, and can therefore be seen as marking the beginning or end of journeys and as the place to receive offerings appropriate to those journeys. In symbolic terms they are also bastions of the faith standing at the boundary between the town and the outside world.

Churches do not seem to have been a prime consideration in the layout of planned medieval towns. In the three medieval boroughs of North Wales, Conwy church was adapted from an earlier monastery and stands in the centre of the town; Beaumaris church stands on the highest ground at the edge of the town; and Caernarfon St Mary stands against the town wall and supplemented an earlier parish church at Llaneblig near the Roman fort. In each case, however, the town is dominated by its fortress.

After the Great Fire of 1666 ambitious plans were drawn up for the redevelopment of London. Wren's plan envisaged replacing 87 burned churches with a mere 25, and advocated building a cemetery outside the city. Churches were to be built on compact sites at focal points in the city. It was not possible to implement the plan, and it has never been possible to undertake urban re-planning of an old city on this scale. Rebuilding took place mainly on the site of destroyed earlier churches. Therefore, in London churches continued to follow the grain of the city they inhabit. Occasionally re-planning of towns has made the most of earlier buildings. Taunton (Somerset) is a good example where the creation in the eighteenth century of Hammet Street provided a vista from the market place that led the eye to the finest of England's church towers. Or re-planning can detract from the setting of a church. Kidderminster's main parish church has been severed from the town by a dual-carriageway ring road, one of the most brutal acts of post-war urban planning.

12 The tower of Bristol St John the Baptist stands over the city gate. It has statues of Brennus and Bellinus, legendary founders of the city, accompanied by the arms of the City and Merchant Venturers. Above, in the centre, is the Stuart Royal Arms

Church building followed the growth of towns; it was not an integral part of it. In 1711 Parliament created a Commission for building 50 new churches in the suburbs of London, but the position of the 11 churches built on new sites was constrained by the availability and cost of land. Five of them were built by Nicholas Hawksmoor, who had ideas very different from Wren. At Spitalfields, Greenwich, Limehouse, Bloomsbury and St George-in-the-East the churches are not hemmed in by adjacent secular buildings, but are allowed to stand free in a dignified grandeur. This has subsequently become the accepted approach to urban church planning.

London was the only city to benefit from a planned programme of church building, albeit a modest one. Among other cities, Birmingham was comparatively well-provided with Anglican places of worship by the end of the eighteenth century. Donation of land allowed chapels-of-ease to be built on the edge of the expanding city but, in common with all major cities, the subsequent population explosion – Birmingham's population rose from about 50,000 in 1780 to over 230,000 half a century later – left the city seriously deficient in Anglican places of worship. One of the problems lay in the reform of ancient parish boundaries, which would result in the loss of parishioners and revenue for many rural parishes where the church was in the wrong place to serve the new population.

In a few cases the church was an integral part of a planned settlement, although the outstanding example of this, at Saltaire (West Yorkshire), is a village with a Congregational chapel rather than a church. Tremadog (Gwynedd) was laid out in the early years of the nineteenth century, but its church stands deliberately apart, in a large churchyard and oriented on a different axis to the streets, giving the impression that it had been there long before the town was built.

4

ARCHITECTURE

In most parish churches in England and Wales it is work of the fifteenth and sixteenth centuries, and of the nineteenth century, that predominates. Although there is very little Anglo-Saxon architecture that remains standing, the earliest period of church building has been intensively studied, partly because there *is* so little of it standing and because much has been learned over recent decades by the opportunity to excavate church sites. Study of the earliest churches is also important because it was at this time that a general plan of the buildings was worked out that has persisted ever since.

Many of the surviving Anglo-Saxon churches, and most of the most interesting ones, were originally monastic churches that later acquired parish status. In other words they were originally churches of higher status than the estate and field churches. The heritage is never a representative sample of the past, an imbalance that seems to increase with age. Anglo-Saxon architecture is not an exception to the rule. Most of the smaller Anglo-Saxon churches were much simpler than the buildings described here, but that does not mean that they were all severe and rudimentary in appearance. Today Monkwearmouth (County Durham) church would be appreciated for its simplicity, but in the eighth century it was highlighted by Bede for its opulence, furnished with pictures and holy relics brought from Rome.

The first Christian places of worship in Britain were mainly single-celled structures, modelled on and easily confused with mausoleums and *cella*, single-celled Roman temples. By the eighth century churches conformed to a basic two-celled structure of a nave for the worshippers and a chancel for the priest, respectively a secular and a sacred space (*13*).

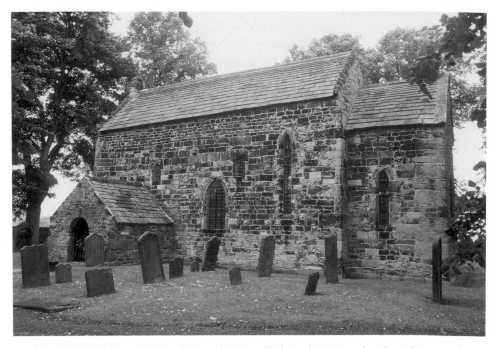

13 Escomb (County Durham) is small two-celled Anglo-Saxon church with unusual square-ended chancel. The tall, narrow proportions of the building are characteristic of the period

This has remained the fundamental division within the church. In these early churches it is uncertain whether the altar was placed at the end of the nave or the east end of the chancel.

Wood was the primary material of construction. The technology of masonry construction had been lost following the end of Roman rule. It was re-introduced in the seventh century but not until the eleventh century did masonry buildings, and the exploitation of quarries to serve them, become common. There was a long period of overlap when timber and masonry were both current, and it should not automatically be assumed that timber was considered to be an inferior material. It was used after the Conquest – the best-surviving early timber church is Greensted (Essex), on the edge of Epping Forest, whose nave has been dated by dendrochronology to the late eleventh century, in other words after the Anglo-Saxon period.

In two-celled churches the chancel was usually semi-circular or polygonal in plan, known as an apse. Most churches were of this type, although in scale they could be tall enough to warrant a clerestorey (an upper tier of windows). Many of the surviving Anglo-Saxon churches included separate side chambers, which were known as a porticus, and were used as a sacristy or vestry, as a place for burial, baptism, or as side chapels. West porticus were often used as porches. Porticus are the precursors of transepts and the cruciform plan. Even small Anglo-Saxon churches might take this form. Bishopstone (Sussex) was an episcopal manor on which a small church was built in the early ninth century. It had porticus to the north and south. A slightly later example can be seen at Britford (Wiltshire), the interior of which retains an enriched arch from the nave.

The most ambitious Anglo-Saxon churches followed the plan of the Roman basilica. The basilican plan, derived from Roman meeting halls, had a nave flanked by aisles set apart by a row of columns, an apse at the east end, and at the west end a triple-celled antechamber known as the narthex. Late seventh-century Northumbrian churches at Hexham and Jarrow (c.684-5) had long narrow naves flanked by rows of porticus, effectively like aisles. This scheme of quasi-aisles was followed on a much more ambitious scale at Brixworth (Northamptonshire), which was founded as a monastic church in the late seventh century, although the present building may belong to the following century (14). Its original arcades of round arches now form the exterior walls, but originally they opened to a series of porticus, one for each bay, showing a transitional phase between the use of the porticus and the creation of an aisle proper by piercing the dividing walls between each cell. A fully developed basilican plan has been argued for Cirencester (Gloucestershire) church, built in the early ninth century but later rebuilt.

Crypts were built in some of the higher-status Anglo-Saxon churches, for the purpose of displaying holy relics or as mausoleums. Some of those churches were later parish churches. Hexham (Northumberland) was built by St Wilfrid c.705 and, although the original basilican church was said to have been destroyed by the Vikings, the original crypt has survived. It forms an extensive range of barrel-vaulted chambers imitating the Roman catacombs and intended for the deposition of relics. Brixworth crypt is in the form of a semi-circular corridor below the outer side of the apse, following the form of the crypt built c.600 at St Peter's in Rome. The crypt at Repton (Derbyshire) is an exceptional survivor and an exceptional work of architecture. In its final form it probably dates to the mid-ninth century and the burial of St Wigstan, who enjoyed cult status in the late Anglo-Saxon period. It has vaults on four round columns decorated with spirals.

14 At Brixworth (Northamptonshire) the original arcade of round arches opened to individual chambers, or porticus, that have since been demolished. The west porticus forms the lower stages of the tower, seen here with a doorway from the nave superimposed by two tiers of openings in the tower

The main focus of architectural expression was on the west side of the building. Churches faced east, and so an approach from the west was logical. West porticus were sometimes of two storeys, although lower than the nave gable. According to Bede, Monkwearmouth church was built in 675 by Frankish masons for Benedict Biscop, who had studied the monastic life in Rome and Lerins. Before 716 a three-bay west porticus had been added, of which only the central chamber has survived. In this central chamber, now forming the two lower stages of the tower, sculpted ornament is visible in the form of panels and a band of animal ornament. The entrance arch is wider than a mere doorway and suggests a symbolic portal. The whole composition was an imposing screen that framed the entrance to the church. Deerhurst (Gloucestershire) is a ninth-century church with an enriched west porticus. It has portals to the exterior, between porticus and nave, and across the centre of the porticus, above which is a sculpture of the Virgin and Child. In other words the entrance to the church was framed by a sequence of three arches.

Brixworth had a screen façade even more ambitious than that at Monkwearmouth, but the only portion that survives is the central chamber that now forms the lower portion of the tower.

A natural development of the west porticus was to heighten it to form a west tower, of which Brixworth, Deerhurst and Monkwearmouth are prime examples. Towers are a feature of Anglo-Saxon stone churches from the tenth century. They are a conspicuous symbol of the power of the church and its patrons, and in symbolic terms had overtones of the heavenly Jerusalem. They had practical functions as well. The upper stage housed the bells that became a familiar feature in the tenth century. The lower stage might be a porch, or possibly a chapel with its own altar. If the tower was three stages high the second stage might also house an altar, or it might have provided access to a gallery in the nave, an early form of private pew.

Contemporary illustrations show that spires also existed at this date, although none have survived. The earliest surviving Anglo-Saxon church tower, built *c.*920, is at Barnack (Huntingdonshire), a two-stage structure under a roof that was taken down when the tower was heightened a

15 Brigstock (Northamptonshire) retains its Anglo-Saxon tower, with characteristic long-and-short work at the angles. The tower was later heightened and a stair turret was added to the west front

century later. Barton-on-Humber (Lincolnshire) has a three-stage tower of *c.*1000, which might have supported a spire, although this too was taken down when a new bell stage was added in the eleventh century. Originally it was the nucleus of the church with a porticus on the east side forming the chancel, and one on the west housing a font.

Most early towers, which also include Brigstock (Northamptonshire) and Bywell (Northumberland), were west towers (*15, 16*). At Barton-on-Humber mentioned above and at Earls Barton (Northamptonshire) the lower stage of the tower was the nave (*17*). In the eleventh century there was also a fashion for central towers at the east end of the nave, following a trend originating with higher-status churches. Durham Cathedral, for example, had both central and western towers by the second quarter of the eleventh century. So did the parish church at Castro in Dover, although the western tower is a reconstituted Roman lighthouse. Breamore (Hampshire) has one of the few surviving central Saxon towers, although it was heightened later in the medieval period.

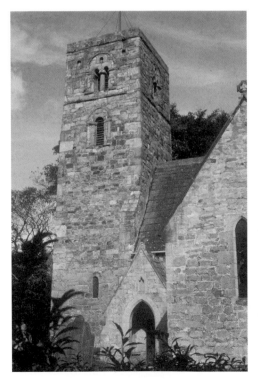

16 The west tower at Bywell (Northumberland) was built in two phases. The lower stage was possibly originally a porch, to which the upper stages were added in the late eleventh century – in date post-Conquest, but in style pre-Conquest

17 Earls Barton
(Northamptonshire) tower was
built in the eleventh century. It
is characteristic of Anglo-Saxon
architecture with its long-and-
short work to the angles, surface
decoration of string courses,
pilaster strips, arches and triangular
heads, and small, round bell
openings

Towers were a focus of architectural enrichment that was also applied
to other parts of the building. Although built of rubble stone the corner
stones, or quoins, were of larger regular blocks laid in a familiar pattern,
the self-explanatory long-and-short work. Wall surfaces were decorated
with raised bands and vertical strips (known as pilaster strips), sometimes
in patterns of blind arcading. The style is perhaps best represented at
Barton-on-Humber and Earls Barton (*17*). It has often been interpreted
as deriving from timber construction, but pilasters, string courses and
arches are all part of the masonry tradition.

The style can also been seen on the nave and chancel. At Bradford-
on-Avon (Wiltshire) the small chapel of St Lawrence was not the
parish church but was probably built to serve a small nunnery after King
Aethelred granted it to Shaftesbury Abbey in 1001. It has masonry of
especially high quality in the form of pilaster strips to the ground storey, above which is a string course and an arcade of blind round arches
that show a mature appreciation of Roman masonry architecture. Wing
(Buckinghamshire) has a simpler but still impressive scheme of pilaster
strips forming an arcade of round arches to its polygonal apse.

18 At Deerhurst (Gloucestershire) the west wall of the nave shows a blocked doorway from the second stage of the west porticus that probably opened to a gallery. Above are two pedimented openings on fluted pilasters, a notional form of classical pediment that reveals the reliance of Anglo-Saxon architecture on Roman buildings

As for other architectural features, early round arches, with thick raised impost blocks on square piers or responds, are little different from re-used Roman arches. Narrow windows also had round heads, or else triangular heads of worked stone that were probably intended as a simplified form of the classical pediment. In some cases, like those on the tower at Deerhurst (Gloucestershire), the jambs are fluted, another indication of the link between Roman and Saxon architecture (*18*). This is more direct at places like Corbridge (Northumberland), when Roman masonry was dismantled and rebuilt as part of the church (*19*). Roofs of timber construction carried thatch roofs, although in no case do they survive.

NORMAN CHURCHES

In contrast to the Anglo-Saxon period, churches that have some surviving Norman features are numerous. The proliferation of church building

19 At Corbridge (Northumberland) the arch leading from the porch is a re-used Roman arch brought from the ruins of the adjacent town

after 1066 has been called a great rebuilding. It included the rebuilding of most of England's cathedrals, the foundation of numerous abbeys, and rebuilding and new building of parish churches. Although this new wave of building more or less coincided with the Norman Conquest it was not a direct product of it. There also was a considerable overlap in architectural style. 'Anglo-Saxon' is used as a dating term, but the term also conveys an architectural style that persisted after the Conquest, since masons continued to build in the manner familiar to them. Wittering (Northamptonshire), Wareham (Dorset), and the towers of Bywell and Monkwearmouth, mentioned above, are good examples of post-Conquest 'Anglo-Saxon' buildings. Other churches, like Milborne Port (Somerset), have features that are Anglo-Saxon in character but have Norman influences.

A revival in architecture, and with it the absorption of continental influences, had been underway from the mid-tenth century, notably in the rebuilding by Edward the Confessor of Westminster Abbey. Before 1100 rebuilding had started, on a vast scale never before seen, at St Paul's in London, Durham, Winchester and Ely Cathedrals, and at St Albans and Bury St Edmunds abbeys. The new style featured arcades of round-headed arches, finely detailed carved ornamentation to both interior and exterior, monumental sculpture and stone vaults. As William of Malmesbury wrote, *c.*1125, it was a 'style which now all seek to emulate at vast expense'.

In parish churches the simple two-cell plan of nave and chancel remained common. Three-celled churches were also built in which the chancel was subdivided and included a separate sanctuary. Kilpeck, Moccas and Peterchurch (the latter four cells and all in Herefordshire), Birkin (North Yorkshire), Steetley Chapel (Derbyshire) and Stewkley

20 Edlingham (Northumberland) has a simple late twelfth-century nave arcade. Round piers carry broad capitals and square abaci that support the round arches

(Buckinghamshire) are all examples of this type. From the twelfth century there was a greater proliferation of nave aisles in new and added to old parish churches, made possible by masons' increasing skill in the construction of arches for arcades (20). Aisles in parish churches were built to allow additional chapels at the east end, or could be built to accommodate more people. Equally, aisles appear to have been added because they had become fashionable and invested the church with more grandeur. Aisles may be among the first architectural expressions of popular piety and local pride.

In towns Norman churches were often larger and aisles were built as a matter of course. Hemel Hempstead and Northampton St Peter retain fine examples of aisled Norman naves with clerestoreys. Hemel Hempstead is cruciform in plan, with vaulted chancel, probably indicating that it had been a minster. The cruciform plan with transepts became common in the Norman period although it existed in England before the Conquest. Great Paxton (Cambridgeshire) and Stow (Lincolnshire), begun in the 1050s, both had full transepts and crossing towers.

Architectural decoration is one of the defining characteristics of Norman churches. An exceptional group of churches in this respect was built in Herefordshire by the Norman rulers of the Welsh Marches. These men built castles to establish their secular domination of the region, founded monasteries to show religious leadership, and built lavish parish churches for the care of their souls, as an expression of their own piety and sophistication, and perhaps also to act as symbols of Norman culture. Kilpeck is the most famous of these churches, although a church of equal quality at Shobdon was demolished in 1752, its portals having been set up as a feature in a landscape park. Kilpeck was built by Hugh of Kilpeck next to his castle, and was complete by 1134. To some extent its construction was traditional: the nave and chancel have the same tall, narrow proportions characteristic of Anglo-Saxon churches. In other respects it is significantly different. It has a two-celled chancel, comprising a square plan section and a narrower apse that is stone vaulted. Its dome-like appearance was a reference to the canopy over the shrine of St Peter in St Peter's Rome and, although rare, was by no means unique in Norman churches with wealthy patrons. Vaulted apses are also at Checkendon, Padworth and Swyncombe (all Oxfordshire), Copford (Essex) which was a chapel of the Bishop of London, Old Bewick (Northumberland) and Fritton (Suffolk).

21 The Sheila-na-gig is the best-known of the grotesque figures on the corbel table at Kilpeck (Herefordshire) and is a symbol of earthly pleasures

Externally Kilpeck features a lavish corbel table – a row of small stone sculptures or mouldings at eaves level – a feature usually only seen in larger churches (*21*). The south doorway is also a richly decorated symbolic threshold, featuring a semi-circular stone tympanum surrounded by outer orders of animals and grotesque faces, and creatures from the *Bestiaries* in circular medallions (*colour plate 2*). The church is among the earliest examples of the book of beasts and their allegorical tales being used in medieval art.

The interior is comparatively plain, emphasis being placed on the chancel arch and the ribs of the sanctuary vault over the altar. The chancel arch represented the important divide between the secular and sacred parts of the church, and at Kilpeck is ornamented with superimposed sculptures of saints and/or priests, one of whom can be identified as St Peter (*22*). Superimposed figures, which also feature on the south doorway, are exceptional features for their date, derived probably from examples in western France.

Architectural elaboration at Kilpeck is found at other Norman churches. The west front was often the most richly detailed, representing as it did the symbolic if not the practical entrance to the church. Iffley (Oxfordshire) was built in the final quarter of the twelfth century, and has a three-celled plan of chancel, tower and nave. Its west front, partially restored in the nineteenth century, is nevertheless well preserved. It has

22 One of the superimposed figures
on the chancel arch at Kilpeck is
St Peter, an outstanding and rare
example of architectural sculpture in a
Norman parish church

23 Castor (Huntingdonshire) has
a fine and well-detailed Norman
crossing tower of the early twelfth
century. The arcading is outlined by
billet friezes and hood moulds, and
above the arches is diamond-pattern
and fish-scale pattern masonry. The
parapet and spire are later

a triple-arched entrance portal, above which is a round window reintro-duced in the nineteenth century, and triple round-headed windows in the gable. Openings are defined by zig-zag, or chevron, mouldings and rows of birds' heads, known as 'beak-head'. Stewkley (Buckinghamshire) has a similar but much simpler west front. Also a three-celled church, Stewkley has a central tower enriched by an arcade of intersecting arches, a favourite motif of Norman masons. Castor (Huntingdonshire) is argu-ably the best-preserved Norman church tower, featuring two stages of arcading with round-headed arches on round shafts (*23*). An earlier tower of the late eleventh century at Sompting (Sussex) has a distinctive Rhenish helm roof, but in its present form dates to rebuilding in the fourteenth century (*24*).

The focus of external elaboration was usually the doorway. Kilpeck is again exceptional (*colour plate 2*). Round arches were constructed of one or more orders of moulding, usually corresponding to the number of shafts flanking the doorway. Kilpeck has only one order of shafts and two orders of mouldings, Barfreston (Kent) two orders of shafts and three orders of mouldings (*25*).

24 Sompting (Sussex) has a fine late eleventh-century tower with a rare Rhenish helm roof. In its present form the roof dates to the fourteenth century, but it may be a copy of the original

25 Barfreston (Kent) is one of England's most richly decorated small Norman churches. Above the south door is a tympanum with the central figure of Christ, and the arch that frames it is decorated with signs of the zodiac and Labours of the Months

Kilpeck and Barfreston are two of many churches whose doorways had a semi-circular tympanum above the door. The iconography of their low-relief carvings is varied. It includes Biblical scenes and other religious subjects such as Christ in Majesty, saints such as George slaying the dragon, less easily interpreted schemes like the Tree of Life, and mythical or imaginary scenes such as fighting monsters (*26, colour plate 3*). In other words, they can refer to the spiritual world within the church, or the sinful world without.

The focus of the interior was invariably the western face of the chancel arch. Arches, treated in a similar fashion to the doorways, were larger and consequently more imposing. Tickencote (Rutland) has a chancel arch of six orders and is very heavy in appearance. Architectural elaboration was otherwise mainly confined to the nave arcades, which feature cylindrical columns that are finished off by various forms of capitals, above which are the flat slabs, known as abaci, from which the round arches spring (*27*). The characteristic moulding of Norman arches is chevron decoration. Northampton St Peter was rebuilt in the mid–twelfth

26 At Stretton Sugwas (Herefordshire) the tympanum has been moved inside the church. Its style and subject – Samson rending the lion's jaws – owes much to similar work in south-west France that was seen by its patron, Oliver de Merlimond, on a pilgrimage to Santiago de Compostella

27 Melbourne (Derbyshire) was built in the early twelfth century, possibly as a
private chapel for Henry I. Its nave arcade and upper tier of arches (known as a
tribune) are the embodiment of the Norman style and its French influence

century on the site of a Saxon church. Its lavish arcade capitals have an
array of birds, faces, foliage and monsters that show just how exuberant
and intricate Norman carving could be. In other important Norman
churches the finest work is to be found in the chancel. Devizes St John
(Wiltshire) was built by Roger of Salisbury, Chancellor to Henry I, in
*c.*1130. It has a vaulted chancel, a sanctuary of intersecting round arches
against the back and side walls, all with chevron moulding, and an east
window with similar decoration to the interior reveals.

EARLY ENGLISH AND DECORATED

The transition from Norman to Gothic architecture was achieved gradually from the final quarter of the twelfth century and into the thirteenth
century. There was a Transitional period encompassing two related but
separate developments: firstly, significant technological advance in the

form of the pointed arch and the pointed rib vault; and second, a new architectural aesthetic. Pointed arches, composed of intersecting arcs, are stronger than round arches because they are better able to withstand vertical and horizontal thrusts. Stone vaulting had little direct relevance to parish churches in the twelfth century, since few parishes could afford such a luxury. Masons learned the technical lessons of the pointed arch and rib vault on larger churches and then applied them to parish churches. But a pointed arch does not necessarily mean a Gothic arch. Where a pointed arch stands on round piers and is decorated with chevron mouldings typical of the twelfth century, it is Transitional. In practice, there was a period in which round and pointed arches were

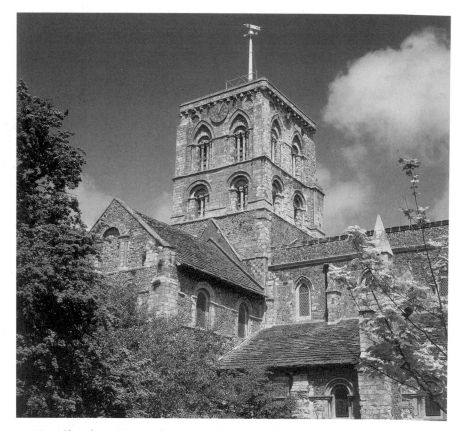

28 New Shoreham (Sussex) has an ambitious church, partly destroyed in the Civil War. The east end, including the tall square tower, was built in the late twelfth century and stylistically is in the Transitional phase between Norman and Gothic. The tower has both round and pointed arches

used in various combinations in the same building, as at Walsoken (Cambridgeshire) and New Shoreham (Sussex). The latter was originally a cruciform parish church but the nave has been mostly taken down (*28*). Its chancel and tower incorporate both pointed and round-headed windows. The long chancel, now used as the nave, has an arcade of alternate round and octagonal piers, and pointed arches with chevron mouldings, under a slightly later rib vault. Walsoken, Long Sutton (Lincolnshire) and Tilney All Saints (Norfolk) are three neighbouring late twelfth-century churches that also have arcades that incorporate alternate round and octagonal piers (*29*).

After the spate of parish church building in Norman England, there were comparatively few new churches built in the thirteenth century. Most Early English work in parish churches comprises rebuilding and enlargement of earlier churches. Early English, the first Gothic style, is a linear form in which ornament is subordinated to the building's structural elements.

29 Walsoken (Cambridgeshire) was built in the final quarter of the twelfth century. The arcades have round arches but the chancel arch is pointed, anticipating the Gothic style

30 Eaton Bray (Bedfordshire) preserves its thirteenth-century architecture to a remarkable degree. The earlier south arcade has octagonal piers and foliage capitals. The more confident north arcade has clustered shafts and stiff-leaf capitals

Where Norman arches display a wide repertoire of decorative schemes, such as chevrons or beak-head friezes, Early English was a series of sharply cut rolls and hollows, using more abstract decoration for the outer orders. These include friezes of pyramid shape known as nailhead, or similar but hollowed-out shapes known as dogtooth. Capitals that are carved with naturalistic looking flowers, known as stiff leaf and resembling daffodils, are characteristic of the Early English style. Brought to perfection at Wells Cathedral, the parish church of Wells St Cuthbert (Somerset) has an arcade with a fine series of stiff-leaf capitals, but also capitals which are more simply moulded and were probably the blanks from which the foliage carvings were sculpted. Where Norman arches had plain round piers, Early English piers were round but were often formed of clustered shafts, like Eaton Bray (Bedfordshire) (*30*). In some cases detached shafts were used. The mid-thirteenth-century church at West Walton (Norfolk) is a tour de force of Early English architecture. In its nave arcades each pier has four detached shafts (originally of local Alwalton marble, but replaced in Purbeck marble) and lavish stiff-leaf capitals (*31, 32*).

31 West Walton (Norfolk) is an outstanding Early English church. The nave arcades feature stiff-leaf capitals, detached marble shafts (replaced in wood) and shaft rings, all classic features of the thirteenth-century style

32 The rich stiff-leaf capitals at West Walton

In its tower, West Walton also exhibits another characteristic feature of Early English architecture, especially in eastern England: the fondness for covering a wall with blind arcading (*33, 34*). It epitomises the abstract and linear approach to decoration.

Some changes in the general structure of parish churches also occurred in the thirteenth and fourteenth centuries. Although the form of churches did not change, towers were given spires of stone, wood or lead, sometimes built on to earlier towers (*35*). Most have since been rebuilt or replaced, but there are a surprising number of surviving spires with medieval fabric. At Chesterfield (Derbyshire) the warped wood and lead spire of the 1360s, only the upper part of which is twentieth-century restoration, is testament to the durability of these materials. There was also a fashion in the thirteenth and fourteenth centuries for octagonal towers. Uffington (Oxfordshire) and North Curry (Somerset) have simple octagonal towers on square bases, and originally had spires. Nantwich

33 West Walton has one of the few detached towers in an English parish church. Built *c.*1240 it is a tour de force of the Early English style with its blank arcading and heavy clasping buttresses

34 Hedon (East Riding) was a major port in the Middle Ages, which is reflected in the scale of its surviving parish church. The north transept is Early English, with external blind arcading typical of the period and of eastern England

(Cheshire) is a more ambitious fourteenth-century tower. Each of these examples demonstrates how the octagonal plan is much better suited to the crossing towers of cruciform churches than to west towers. A later octagonal west tower at Coxwold (North Yorkshire) is by comparison awkward in its relationship with the nave. A fashion for detached towers was more localised, having been favoured on the borders of Norfolk, Lincolnshire and Cambridgeshire. West Walton is the supreme example (*33*), Wisbech (Cambridgeshire) another, while an example of the tradition persisting to the later Middle Ages is at Terrington St Clement (Norfolk). They demonstrate how towers were built as an outward statement about the church and were not integrated with the internal workings of the building. The concept of the tower as a statement in its own right helps to explain what at first appear to be over-sized towers built in the later Middle Ages, especially in Somerset.

35 At Long Sutton (Lincolnshire) the early Gothic tower was originally detached from the body of the church. Slightly later than the tower it is one of the best-preserved medieval spires

During the thirteenth century the first effigies were sculpted for parish churches, and to accommodate them it was sometimes necessary to construct arched recesses in the nave walls. Windows became larger in the thirteenth century, and were of the lancet type (in which the arch is made up of two arcs, the radius of which is greater than the arch span). Window tracery was formed when two or three lancets were placed together and the spaces between the tops of the lancets had small round lights cut through the wall. This is known as plate tracery. The next development was to produce bar tracery: this comprised a single larger window into which two or three main lights were separated by thin stone mullions, which were continued above to form the round tracery lights. Bar tracery appears in parish churches towards the end of the thirteenth century, what the Victorians would describe as the geometrical style. In its original late thirteenth-century form it can be appreciated in

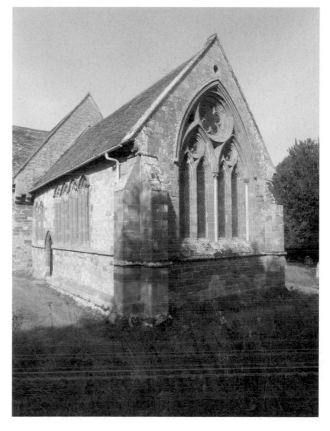

36 Acton Burnell (Shropshire) was built in the late thirteenth century by Robert Burnell, Bishop of Bath and Wells. Its has a particularly fine chancel with state-of-the-art features like early bar tracery

the chancels that were not enlarged in the later Middle Ages. Ile Abbots (Somerset) has a fine thirteenth-century chancel with bar tracery in its windows, although the rest of the church is much later. Acton Burnell (Shropshire) was built by Robert Burnell, bishop of Bath and Wells, and has original bar-tracery windows and windows of two and four main lights divided by mullions, but without tracery (*36*).

Development of window tracery was one of the chief characteristics of the Decorated style, a period that covers the first half of the fourteenth century, at least until the Black Death of 1348. Masons quickly gained confidence in building windows with bar tracery, which now were larger and were transformed into a variety of patterns. Development of the ogee, or S-shaped arch, and use of triangles composed of three arcs (known as spheric triangles) are two of the innovations in window tracery that enabled novel forms of curvaceous patterns to evolve (*37*).

37 Decorated architecture brought innovation in the design of window tracery, with many fine examples in Lincolnshire churches, such as the flowing tracery at Holbeach

As its name suggests, the Decorated style is concerned with decoration and style more than structure, and its motifs such as ogee arches and foliage decoration are to be found on architecture and in the applied arts such as painting, metalwork and ivory carving. It is also a period when stained glass, shrines, tombs and new liturgical furniture were introduced, augmenting the richness of the interior. The plainness of some churches compared to the opulence of others reveals a growing gap in wealth between regions and individuals. From the early fourteenth century the super-rich built some of the finest buildings in England, including the churches of St Mary Redcliffe in Bristol, Winchelsea (Sussex) and Patrington (East Riding).

Heckington (Lincolnshire) church was built by both lay and ecclesiastical benefactors, representing the different tastes of Richard

38 Higham Ferrers (Northamptonshire) has a large town church mainly built in the thirteenth and fourteenth centuries. Its parapet spire is characteristic of the fourteenth century

de Postegrave, its priest, and Isabella de Vesci, its lay patron. Its exterior is an almost unaltered essay in the Decorated style, with exceptional chancel fittings that are described later. St Mary Redcliffe, a church of twelfth-century origin built outside the city walls, was rebuilt from the mid-fourteenth century and exhibits many of the preoccupations of contemporary architects. Its nave is so tall it needs flying buttresses. On the north side it has a hexagonal porch, an experiment in planning that can also be seen in the polygonal spaces at Ely and Wells Cathedrals. The decoration at St Mary Redcliffe is opulent, especially the exotic detail of the porch, for which Indian and Islamic influences have been suggested, expressing the cosmopolitan nature of Bristol, then the nation's second port. Patrington, built on the profits of the wool trade, is a church almost entirely of the Decorated period. It has a conventional

cruciform plan with a crossing tower and spire, but on a grand scale for a parish church, and has much of the fashionable architectural detail than can be seen in the richer wool churches of Yorkshire, Lincolnshire and East Anglia. Its arcades have diamond-shaped piers with clustered shafts, and rich foliage capitals; its original windows have striking tracery designs and the church has vaulted chantry chapel and aisles (*39, colour plate 4*). As a whole, Patrington church expresses perhaps better than any other the ideal of the parish church as it was envisaged in the fourteenth century.

Vaults remained rare in parish churches, although they were near universal in churches of higher status, where patterns had developed far beyond the rib vaults of the Early English. St Mary Redcliffe is vaulted throughout. Its porch has a vault including subsidiary ribs that do not spring from the walls, known as liernes, forming a star pattern (*40*). The high vaults of the nave and chancel are later fourteenth-century work, in the transition between Decorated and Perpendicular styles. Ottery St Mary (Devon) was built by Bishop Grandison of Exeter from 1337 as a chantry for himself and his family, and also features lierne vaults, enriched by sculpted figures on the bosses. However, these churches are exceptional; wooden roofs remained the norm in parish churches.

Opposite: 39 A foliage capital in the nave arcade at Patrington (East Riding)

Right: 40 St Mary Redcliffe, Bristol, is one of the most ambitious parish churches in England. It has an innovative fourteenth-century octagonal porch with a star vault

PERPENDICULAR AND TUDOR GOTHIC

The Perpendicular style that became established by the end of the four-teenth century remained in vogue up until the Reformation and beyond. Tudor Gothic refers to the variation of the style that emerged at the end of the fifteenth century and included square-headed windows and broader, shallow four-centred arches. This period was a golden age for parochial church architecture, at a time when there was comparatively little work undertaken at cathedrals and monasteries, at least compared to what had gone before. As has already been pointed out, in a medieval parish church the lay community was responsible for the secular parts of the church, while the patrons remained responsible for the chancel. With their increasing prosperity lay communities set about rebuilding and refurnishing their churches in an outpouring of popular piety and local pride. One consequence of this is that in many cases a lofty Perpendicular nave is joined to an older, lower and smaller chancel, whose patrons could not or would not rebuild in a style to suit the remainder of the church. In some churches, therefore, like Leigh-on-Mendip (Somerset), the chan-cel looks pitifully small against the nave and tower, doing insufficient justice to the importance of the chancel. It was also a period of very large churches

– like Ludlow St Laurence (Shropshire) and Long Melford (Suffolk) among many – that dominated their respective towns and villages.

Advances in building technology and the availability of glass allowed windows in Perpendicular churches to be larger than before. Larger windows made for lighter interiors, a trend influenced by the new mendicant orders of Franciscan and Dominican friars. Their own light-filled preaching churches, like the now destroyed Blackfriars and Greyfriars in London, influenced light-filled early Perpendicular churches like Hedon, Hull Holy Trinity (both East Riding) and Winchelsea (Sussex). Broad windows had four-centred arches (i.e. arches composed of the arcs of four circles), and in the sixteenth century square-headed windows were introduced, although they were more common in secular than ecclesiastical architecture. The style of tracery also changed to an emphasis on vertical mullions, forming regular tracery lights ideal for stained glass figures. Where windows were particularly large the main lights were divided by horizontal transoms. Large windows in walls under embattled parapets with pinnacles,

Above: 1 Stocklinch Ottersey (Somerset) is an isolated church where no trace is now visible of the settlement it once served

Right: 2 The early twelfth-century south doorway at Kilpeck (Herefordshire) has a tympanum with lavish ornamentation showing influences from western France and from the *Bestiaries*, the Book of Beasts. On the right-hand capital is a green man, one of the earliest examples of the figure in an English church

Above: 3 The Norman tympanum at Aston Eyre (Shropshire) depicts Christ's entry into Jerusalem

Left: 4 Patrington (East Riding) is one of the finest Decorated churches in eastern England and is almost entirely of one period. The arcades, with octagonal piers and a band of foliage forming the capital, is typical of the mid fourteenth century

Right: 5 The sixteenth-century tower of North Petherton (Somerset) is one of the best-conceived and richly ornamented towers in Britain

Below: 6 Gresford (Denbighshire) has a rich panelled roof carried on cambered tie beams

7 One of the finest late medieval wagon roofs is at Collumpton (Devon)

8 The double hammerbeam roof at March (Cambridgeshire) is one of the masterpieces of medieval carpentry and is one of the exemplary cases where the roof of the church is like looking up to heaven and its company of angels

9 Ingestre (Staffordshire) is Sir Christopher Wren's one provincial church. The chancel screen by Grinling Gibbons is surmounted by the Arms of Charles II

10 Shobdon (Herefordshire) was built in the eighteenth century to replace a Norman church, with an interior in a consistent picturesque Gothic style

11 Cheadle (Staffordshire) is a Roman Catholic church by A.W.N. Pugin that profoundly influenced the Anglican Revival. The architecture is Decorated style. The decoration, including wall painting and even painting of the arcade piers, was an attempt to recreate an ideal of the medieval church

12 Great Witley (Worcestershire) has an interior scheme by James Gibbs, containing fittings
from a chapel at Cannons, near London, that were sold off in 1747. The painting of the
Resurrection is by Antonio Bellucci. The ceiling is not plasterwork, but constructed by
Italian craftsmen of lighter papier maché

Right: 13 The Doom of *c.*1859 at Highnam (Gloucestershire) is the work of Thomas Gambier Parry, who devised his own spirit-based paint that enabled him to copy Italian fresco techniques

Below: 14 Fairford (Gloucestershire) is the only parish church to retain a complete set of medieval stained glass, made in the early years of the sixteenth century under the direction of Barnard Flower, a Dutch immigrant and the king's glazier. The west window depicts the Day of Judgement

Left: 15 The allegorical east window at Shrewsbury St Alkmund (Shropshire) is by Francis Eginton of Birmingham, installed in 1795 and based on an oil painting by Guido Reni. A figure representing Faith rises from the cross and reaches out for the crown of everlasting life. The cross spans the river of death

Below: 16 Selsley (Gloucestershire) was the first commission for stained glass received by Morris, Marshall, Faulkner & Co. The Annunciation was designed by William Morris, based on a painting by Jan van Eyck

Right: 17 The glass at
Tudeley (Kent) was designed
by Marc Chagall. The
east window, completed
in 1967, commemorates
Sarah Venetia d'Avigdor-
Goldsmid, who drowned
in an accident in 1963. The
window links the turmoil
of the sea and grief with
a ladder leading up to an
angel and the arms of Christ

Below: 18 The coving of
the rood loft at Aymestry
(Herefordshire) is like a
vault in miniature

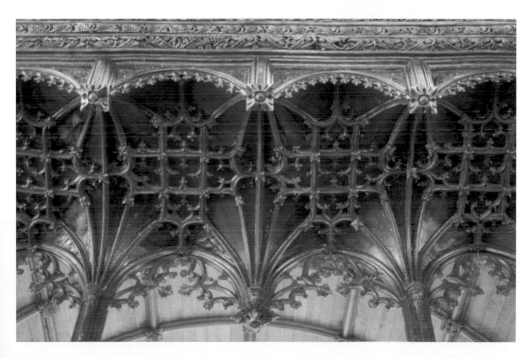

Above: 19 The figure of the archangel Michael on the dado of the rood screen at Ranworth (Norfolk)

Opposite above: 20 The Tomb of Christ of the mid-fourteenth century at Irnham (Lincolnshire) has the intricate carving of the best work of the period

Opposite below: 21 The chalice-shaped font at Eardisley (Herefordshire) is boldly carved with scenes of a duel, Christ's Harrowing of Hell, and a lion. Here two knights duel, impeded by the entangling vegetation. It has been suggested that the duel represents a real event in 1127 at which Sir Ralph de Baskerville slew his father-in-law

22 The benches at Crowcombe (Somerset) are dated 1534. Here two men, tangled in branches spewing from a monster's mouth, grapple with a double-headed wyvern

23 Stanford-on-Avon (Northamptonshire) retains a seventeenth-century organ case. It also has a fine collection of funeral hatchments

24 The tomb of Sir Richard Corbet (died 1567) at Moreton Corbet (Shropshire) has restored paintwork to its heraldic shields, giving an insight into how such tombs originally appeared

25 The monument to Thomas Cave (died 1613) at Stanford-on-Avon (Northamptonshire) is essentially still medieval in the lower section, with recumbent effigies on a tomb chest with weepers. Above, an arch frames Latin inscriptions and the whole piece is surmounted by classical columns with an entablature, and is crowned with heraldic achievements

Opposite: 41 Whiston (Northamptonshire) is a Perpendicular village church with characteristically large windows and an embattled parapet

Right: 42 Terrington St Clement (Norfolk) is a classic large Perpendicular church in a region rich in late medieval buildings

similar to those on towers, characterised the most ambitious Perpendicular churches (*41, 42*). Porches became a showpiece of the church exterior, enriched by figure sculpture in niches. But it was in towers that the architects of Perpendicular churches excelled.

The cruciform plan declined in popularity, with a result that there are few elaborate architectural west fronts. There are exceptions, like Beverley St Mary (East Riding) and Crewkerne (Somerset). If chantry or guild chapels were needed they could easily be added to aisles or chancels, to make a less compact plan than a cruciform church, but one more logical to the building's use. The problem with the cruciform plan was that the crossing arches stood between nave and chancel, inhibiting the view between them. West towers were now much more favoured and in this period the tower became a feature in its own right, without the need for a spire.

Church towers are among the finest sites in English architecture. In Wales too they are an integral part of the landscape and range from the sumptuous towers of Wrexham and Northop (Flintshire) in the prosperous North East to the austere simplicity of Pembrokeshire towers (see *61*). Towers are an extrovert statement of the community and often fostered local rivalries. They show that architecture was not the overlooked art form that it is today, and that a sophisticated aesthetic was not just the preserve of a more cultured elite.

The scale and architectural style of towers is varied. The best are all single compositions. Piecemeal designs are less effective. For example, England's tallest church tower, at Boston (Lincolnshire), is an imposing and unforgettable building but not a great design. The best Perpendicular towers are outstanding works of architecture in their own right, and include those of the East Riding, Cheshire and north-east Wales, Gloucestershire and especially Somerset. These towers were carefully designed to accentuate their vertical emphasis and decoration was controlled from the relatively plain lower stage to the final flourish of the parapet. Most towers are either three or four stages. They have buttresses usually set back from the angles (allowing a greater number of vertical lines to help accentuate verticality), or perhaps set diagonally, the preferred form in the Cotswolds. If it is a west tower then it probably has a west doorway, largely symbolic, and a large west window to light the west end of the nave. Each stage will have one or two windows, with similar bell openings in the upper stage. Most of these have wooden louvres, but in Somerset the towers feature sound holes in the form of pierced stone tracery. Pevsner called it 'Somerset tracery' and the name has stuck. The parapet is usually embattled and incorporates gargoyles and pinnacles. Figure sculpture might originally have been part of the design, but the niches will now be empty or replaced with nineteenth- or twentieth-century figures. Original sculpture has rarely survived. Where it does it can be a disappointment – the otherwise peerless tower at Ile Abbots (Somerset) has figures now badly weathered, but they were never of more than indifferent quality.

Among the earliest Perpendicular square-topped towers was Wells St Cuthbert (Somerset) of *c.*1405, probably by the same architect who designed the cathedral north-west tower, where the concept of a square-topped tower was pioneered. Otherwise the most notable early Perpendicular towers are found further north, especially the group of

43 Hedon is one of the fine group of early Perpendicular towers in the East Riding.
It is strong in design and vertical emphasis but without the ornate treatment of
Tudor period towers

fine towers in the East Riding, such as Howden, Cottingham and Hedon (*43*). These are all crossing towers on older buildings. Another fine early Perpendicular tower at Doncaster (South Yorkshire) was destroyed by fire in 1853.

Somerset towers belong mainly to the late fifteenth and the sixteenth century, and are more richly treated than the East Riding towers. They fall into two distinct stylistic groups, one derived from the Wells Cathedral towers (Batcombe, Bruton, Chewton Mendip, Evercreech, Ilminster, Leigh-on-Mendip, Mells, Wells St Cuthbert) and the other more common in west Somerset (Huish Episcopi, Ile Abbots, Kingsbury Episcopi, Kingston St Mary, North Petherton, Ruishton, Staple Fitzpaine, Taunton St Mary and an outlier in Cornwall at Probus) (*44, colour plate 5*).

Other regions had their own idiosyncrasies. In Gloucestershire blind arcading was favoured in the middle stage, like Chipping Camden (*6*) and Cirencester, following the example set at Gloucester Abbey (now cathedral). Devon towers are characterised by their prominent south stair turrets. In the east Midlands there was briefly a fashion for the tower to

44 The finely detailed sixteenth-century west tower at Huish Episcopi (Somerset) is in the style favoured in the Taunton district

45 Fotheringay (Northamptonshire) was built by master mason William Horwood from 1434. The octagonal lantern on the upper stage of the tower is a feature of contemporary churches in the region, but the flying buttresses in the nave are unusual. The chancel of this former collegiate church was demolished in 1573

46 Altarnun is one of the largest Perpendicular parish churches in Cornwall, with typical simple arcade piers and arches, and arched-brace roofs. The church is also notable for its late medieval benches and has a fine Norman font

be capped by a narrower octagonal stage, or lantern, like the fifteenth-century towers at Boston (Lincolnshire), Lowick and Fotheringay (both Northamptonshire), the latter a collegiate church built from 1434 by the master mason William Horwood (45).

Lightness and space characterise the best Perpendicular interiors. Arcades became broader, on ever more slender piers and with wide four-centred arches (46). Vaulting was still unusual, although it found favour in the square spaces beneath towers and in porches, or was used in chantry chapels. The most characteristic form of late Gothic vaulting is the fan vault, which features radiating ribs, the cells between which are filled with panelling. Somerset has many such tower and porch vaults. The great fan-vaulted churches of Bath and Sherborne Abbeys are now parish churches, but they were originally abbey churches. At Collumpton, the

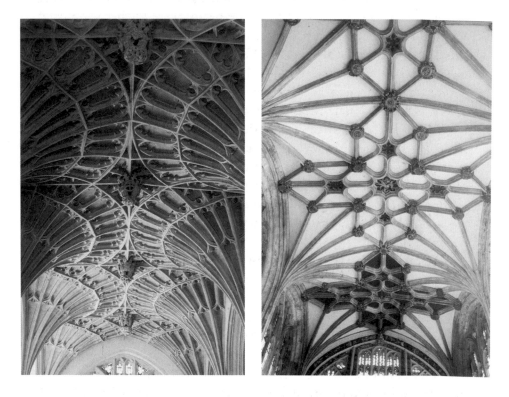

Above left: 47 The fan vault of the Lane aisle at Collumpton (Devon), of the early sixteenth century

Above right: 48 The lierne vault in the Beauchamp chapel at Warwick St Mary aisle built by the wool merchant John Lane *c.*1525 shows how effective fan vaulting could be in comparatively small buildings (*47*). At Warwick St Mary, the Beauchamp chapel, built 1443-75 by Thomas Kerver, has a less-common lierne vault (*48*). In many of these cases vaulting of the private sections of the building was a deliberate contrast with the wooden roofs in the remainder of the church.

It is with wooden roofs that parish churches excel. Wooden roofs should not be regarded as inferior to stone vaulting, especially as wood offered greater scope for carved display than masonry, with a result that surviving church roofs can be found from the simplest to the most sumptuous. The basic structural elements of timber roofs are the tie beam and principal rafters, a triangular shape further strengthened by the use of vertical posts in the centre (king posts) or offset from the centre (queen posts). The principals carry the longitudinal purlins. Instead of resting entirely on the top of the wall, many tie beams were further supported by wall brackets on corbels. Use of subsidiary rafters and purlins enabled the underside of the roof to be formed into a complex grid of square panels, which could be painted or carved. The intersections of the wooden members, or ribs, could be enriched with carved decoration known as bosses. Where roofs had a very flat pitch, for example in relatively narrows aisles, the roof might simply be carried on tie beams, with subsidiary embossed ribs forming square panels. King-post and tie-beam roofs are found in all districts. Somerset has a rich heritage of king-post roofs. The sixteenth century roofs at Somerton and Martock are outstanding, but there are other fine earlier roofs at Bruton, High Ham, Leigh-on-Mendip, Taunton St Mary, Wells St Cuthbert and Weston Zoyland (*49*).

At Somerton the spaces between the king posts and the principal rafters are carved with dragon silhouettes. At Wells St Cuthbert the roof has been repainted and reproduces the general gaily coloured effect that these roofs were originally given. Wiltshire also has roofs of this type, for example at Salisbury St Thomas, and at Bere Regis (Dorset) the roof has prominent enriched arched braces beneath the tie beams. North-east Wales and Cheshire also boast a rich heritage of panelled roofs. At Ruthin and Gresford (both Denbighshire) the shallow-pitched nave roofs have cambered tie beams and rich panelled decoration (*colour plate 6*). Instead of square panels, Blythburgh (Suffolk) has a similar shallow-pitched nave roof, which has closely spaced subsidiary rafters

carried on a ridge beam and one purlin each side, all with painted decoration. The tie beam also carries large carved winged angels, a recurrent motif in East Anglian church roofs, and a reminder that in a medieval church looking up to the roof was akin to looking up towards heaven.

The other main types of roof employed arched braces. Like tie-beam roofs, arched-brace roofs could have subsidiary braces and longitudinal ribs that formed square panels, especially fine examples of which are at Collumpton (Devon) and Shepton Mallet (Somerset) (*colour plate 7*). If the panels are ceiled with plaster, it is known as a wagon roof, the kind most commonly in found in south-west England, where the enrichment was focused on the bosses and on the cornices, often carved with vine trails. The combination of strength and delicacy in wagon roofs is seen at a number of churches like Luccombe, Selworthy and Watchet St Decuman (all Somerset).

To obtain a greater span the arched braces could spring from short projecting beams known as hammerbeams. The first such roof was built in the last decade of the fourteenth century at Westminster Hall, London, and in the late Middle Ages the type found most favour in East Anglia.

Right: 50 Cawston (Norfolk) has
one of the best examples of a late
medieval hammerbeam roof

Opposite: 49 The richly detailed
king-post roof at Weston Zoyland
(Somerset) probably belongs to the
early sixteenth century

Classic examples include Cawston, Outwell, Upwell (all Norfolk), Bury
St Edmunds, Earl Stonham and Needham Market (all Suffolk) (*50*).
Needham Market roof, built in the period 1458-78, is a unique variation
in which the hammerbeams carry tall posts with tie beams, and then
clerestorey windows and a second tier of tie beams. In some East Anglian
churches, of which March (Cambridgeshire) is the best known because
of its array of angels, the roof has two tiers of hammerbeams, although in
such cases the upper hammerbeams are purely decorative as they would
be unable to support the weight of the roof (*colour plate 8*). Other churches,
like Woolpit (Suffolk), Swaffham and Tilney All Saints (both Norfolk) also
have double hammerbeam roofs. A variation found in north-east Wales
was for alternate hammerbeam and arched-brace trusses, of which the
former were decorative rather than structural. Examples are at Llangollen,
Llanfarchell (both Denbighshire) and Cilcain (Flintshire). Mildenhall
(Suffolk) has a similar alternation of hammerbeam and tie-beam trusses.

POST-REFORMATION CHURCHES

Little new church building occurred in the latter half of the sixteenth century, although repairs were carried out and some notable roofs were built during this period. Acton Burnell, dated 1598, and Condover (both Shropshire) have Elizabethan roofs, whereas many undecorated arched-brace roofs like, for example, Aberedw (Powys), might also be of this date. The few new churches built before the second half of the seventeenth century continue the Perpendicular or Tudor-Gothic style, the principal style with which the masons were familiar. Staunton Harold (Leicestershire) was begun in 1653 by Sir Robert Shirley and a foundation inscription explains that Gothic was also a political gesture of the old religion. During the Commonwealth, 'When all things sacred were throughout ye nation either demolisht or profaned Sir Robert Shirley Baronet founded this church whose singular praise it is to have done ye best things in ye worst of times.' Sir Robert died in the Tower of London in 1656.

Architecture was changing significantly during the sixteenth century when the effects of the European Renaissance began to appear, a trend best seen in secular rather than ecclesiastical architecture. A new kind of architecture was needed for the Anglican church, and one in tune with the contemporary emphasis placed upon the pulpit rather than the altar and the sacraments. Inigo Jones (1573-1652) built a new church of St Paul in Covent Garden, London, in 1631 in a primitive Tuscan style derived from his study of the works of Italian architect Palladio (1508-80). From the outside it looks like a temple rather than a church but it was influential in the designs of Anglican churches and dissenting chapels. There was no internal structural division between nave and chancel, the altar being now only a minor fixture. It became a key building in the search for a new style of architecture for the Church of England, what would become known as auditory churches or, less charitably, as preaching boxes. Ironically St Paul dates from Archbishop Laud's revival of some of the Catholic forms of worship. Other early classical-inspired churches, like the remarkable church at Berwick-upon-Tweed (Northumberland) of 1650-2, follow the ground plan of the medieval church (*51*).

The Fire of London in 1666 was to be the impetus for a fresh approach to church architecture. In the subsequent rebuilding Sir Christopher Wren (1632-1723), Nicholas Hawksmoor (1661-1736) and others established Baroque as the dominant architectural style, one that prevailed for

51 Berwick-upon-Tweed (Northumberland) church was built by John Young, a London mason, in 1650-2 and is one of the few important churches built during the Commonwealth. Originally a mixture of Gothic and classical styles, some of the Gothic motifs were replaced by classical ones when it was restored in 1855

over a century. Their use of classical columns, round arches and window heads, and rich plasterwork incorporating standard classical motifs like draped cloths (swags) or fruit and flowers (festoons) are the same motifs that were used in secular architecture. The principal difference is in the structure of the buildings, to which the medieval precedent of a nave with lower and narrower chancel remained important. Sir Christopher Wren's Ingestre (Staffordshire) of *c.*1676 looks like a medieval church in its exterior form, with only the round-headed windows hinting at the classical inspiration of the interior (*colour plate 9*). But the architect's most influential ideas were those that differed from the previously accepted norms. For example, at St Stephen Walbrook Wren adapted the medieval plan to create an unusual square nave, and used Corinthian columns to support round arches beneath a central circular dome. Arches and dome are of wood but plastered with ornate detail. The church steeple also remained important, even though there was no precedent that could be adapted from classical architecture. Wren and Hawksmoor both designed many spires in London, at Spitalfields rising from a temple-like west portico.

Temple-like churches with classical columns and rich plasterwork were designed by other architects working on London churches, like St Mary le Strand of 1714-7 and St Martin in the Fields of 1722 by James Gibbs (1682-1754), and Deptford of 1713-30 by Thomas Archer (1668-1743). Baroque churches appeared in other towns and cities, two notable examples of which are Bristol Christ Church by William Paty of 1786-90, and Northampton All Saints of 1676-80, by Henry Bell, which with its domed nave is remarkably early for an accomplished Wren-like church (52).

Most churches were less opulent, but the classical style was adaptable to modest decoration. In auditory churches the chancel was of diminished importance and so the architects could conceive the church as having a single principal space. Galleries were introduced in the seventeenth century because they increased the capacity of the church, created a more compact theatrical appearance, well suited to a form of worship based on preaching, and improved the acoustics of the church to allow everyone to hear (53).

52 Northampton All Saints was built 1676-80 by Henry Bell. The interior has a central dome supported on Ionic columns, reminiscent of some of Wren's London churches, with plasterwork by Edward Goudge

The single main space also allowed experiments away from the rectangular nave. The central dome carried on columns arranged in a square, of which Wren's St Stephen Walbrook is perhaps the supreme example, has already been mentioned. The later eighteenth century saw a brief flirtation with octagonal and even circular churches. James Gibbs had proposed a 'round design' for St Martin in the Fields, London (1720), but it was not built. George Steuart's Shrewsbury St Chad (1789-92) adopts a circular plan. The shape was chosen specifically because its acoustics allowed the preacher to be well heard in all parts of the building. In this respect church architecture followed a precedent set by other denominations. George Steuart cited the inspiration of some of these, including Edinburgh St Andrew of 1781-7 by Andrew Frazer, and also cited the oval plan of Newcastle-upon-Tyne All Saints of 1786-96 by David Stephenson (converted to offices and auditorium in 1983-84). The octagonal plan was also taken up in a few cases, it having been a favourite form for Methodist churches after John Wesley was impressed with the Congregationalists' Octagon Chapel in Norwich, built in 1754-6. Notable examples of the octagonal form in Anglican

53 The Chapel of King Charles the Martyr at Tunbridge Wells (Kent) was built mainly 1688-96. It has ornate plaster ceilings by Henry Doogood, who had previously worked in London for Wren. The chancel is framed by a round arch with narrower flat-headed openings, known as a serliana. It was also one of the earliest churches to have a gallery

churches are a chapel at Bath (1767 by Timothy Lightoler, later the Royal Photographic Society), and Madeley (Shropshire), built 1793-7 by Thomas Telford (1757-1834) at a noted centre of Methodism.

In the eighteenth century the question of style remained important. A revival of Gothic architecture was part of a Romantic movement that sought the exotic and antique. In architecture it was influenced by *Ancient Architecture Restored* (1741-2) by Batty Langley (1696-1751), a source book for many architects interested in Gothic designs, although Langley's scholarship was not very rigorous. The Gothic (sometimes labelled Gothick) style once again found favour in church design, although it was employed in a purely decorative fashion. Estate churches like Croome d'Abitot (Worcestershire) of 1758 by Capability Brown enhance the picturesque appearance of their respective estates. Another estate church is at Shobdon (Herefordshire), built in 1752 from plans for a 'Rococo Gothic' church sent from London (*colour plate 10*). It uses Gothic motifs in a purely decorative fashion, and its effect relies on the consistency of its application inside the building, for the arches framing the windows, the arches over the chancel and the shaped ends of the pews. Gothic was employed for stronger and less fussy designs, with notable examples in Tetbury (Gloucestershire) of 1777-81 by Francis Hiorne, Kings Norton (Leicestershire) by John Wing the Younger of 1757-75 and Shrewsbury St Alkmund (Shropshire) by John Carline of 1794-5, notable for its early use of cast-iron windows.

A simpler Gothic style was favoured in the early nineteenth century that has often been misleadingly labelled (and derided) as 'Commissioners Gothic'. It was a style well suited to the low-church services that it hosted. The parliamentary grants that kick-started church building in the nineteenth century produced buildings in a range of architectural styles in what should be regarded as an eclectic age. Most of these churches were Gothic but not exclusively so (*54, 55*). Sir Robert Smirke (1780-1867) was the leading architect of the Greek Revival style, and is best known as the architect of the British Museum. But he built several Greek-style churches for the Church Commissioners, as did other architects best known for their secular commissions, like George Basevi (1794-1845), John Nash (1752-1835) and Sir John Soane (1753-1837). A simplified Norman or Romanesque style also found favour, for example in the work of T.H. Wyatt (1807-80) at Glyntaf (Glamorgan) of 1838 and Bethnal Green St Andrew (London) of 1840-1, precursors of his more ambitious church at Wilton (Wiltshire) described below (see *9*).

Above: 54 A brick church was built at the industrial settlement of Ironbridge (Shropshire) in 1836-7 by Thomas Smith, a local builder-architect. The Church Commissioners awarded a grant of £200 out of a total cost of £3,176. Its simple Gothic style was characteristic of the early nineteenth century

Right: 55 Uttoxeter (Staffordshire) was built in 1828 by Trubshaw and Johnson. It is in a Gothic style with integral galleries, an arrangement soon to be disfavoured in the Anglican Revival

VICTORIAN CHURCHES AND THE ANGLICAN REVIVAL

The nineteenth-century revival of Gothic architecture began with individual architects like Thomas Rickman (1776-1841) who became interested in reproducing the forms of medieval churches. Rickman built Commissioners' churches and was also author of *An Attempt to Discriminate the Styles of Architecture in England* (1817), which established the terms Early English, Decorated and Perpendicular. But the most influential advocate of Gothic was A.W.N. Pugin (1812-52). In his book *Contrasts* (1836) he drew unfavourable comparisons between the dull utilitarian buildings of his own day and the glories of the medieval past. Its devastating critique was followed up in *The True Principles of Pointed or Christian Architecture* (1841). Gothic was advocated as the only true style for a Christian building. Classical architecture was dismissed as pagan. Pugin put his ideas into practice, although all of his churches were built for the Roman Catholic faith. He had converted to the Roman Catholic Church in 1834, at a time when it was enjoying a revival following the Catholic Emancipation Act of 1829 that removed all social barriers to Catholicism. Pugin was not the only refugee from the Church of England to feel at home there.

As an idealist, Pugin found it difficult to develop fully his ideas without adequate financial resources. His masterpiece is the lavish Cheadle St Giles (Staffordshire) of 1841-6, where he found a suitably wealthy patron in the Earl of Shrewsbury (*colour plate 11*). The style is Decorated, the most preferred English Gothic style, and its tall, slender spire expresses the importance of verticality in Christian architecture. The interior is treated lavishly, but in a controlled fashion that turned the focus away from the pulpit and sermon toward the chancel and the sacraments. Walls and piers are all painted. Decoration becomes more opulent in the chancel, where the importance of the altar is emphasised by raising it up on steps. Although Pugin had attempted to reconstruct the Middle Ages, he in fact idealised it, one of the defining characteristics of the age. Unlike his medieval counterparts, Pugin was also responsible for the furnishing and decoration of the church. His wall paintings and rood screen contributed as much to the medieval spirit of the building as did the architecture.

Pugin was a man of his time who enjoyed the support of the Tractarians and Ecclesiologists. Within a few years of Cheadle *The Ecclesiologist* journal was giving similar practical advice to the architectural and applied

56 South Dalton (East Riding) was built by J.L. Pearson in 1858-61. The special sanctity of the chancel was expressed here by designing early Gothic blind arcading around the sanctuary

57 Denstone (Staffordshire) of 1860-2 is by G.E. Street and has a chancel taller than the nave. It is one example of how Victorian church architecture expressed the renewed emphasis on the sacraments of the church

arts professions, based on the antiquarian study of medieval churches and a renewed appreciation of their moral and artistic value. From it grew the notion of 'correct' forms of architecture and decoration, including a renewed architectural emphasis on the chancel (56, 57). Soaring spires sprang up in countryside and industrial towns just as Pugin had wanted (58). However, Ecclesiologists were also keen to promote the idea of architecture appropriate for its location. For example, for a small village church simple Early English might be appropriate where Perpendicular or Decorated would be better suit an urban setting. But the rediscovery of medieval architecture was not confined to the native tradition, since French and Italian Gothic and Romanesque architecture also met with enthusiastic approval. Nor was it averse to new building materials. Brick was taken up by many High-Victorian architects, in a period of great creativity when the Gothic Revival displayed all manner of influences from William Butterfield's Italian Gothic and the early French Gothic of Sir Gilbert Scott and William Burges. For a new generation of architects understanding the past was a fundamental part of creating buildings for the future. Architects were also, like Pugin, now much more involved in all aspects of a building, including its furnishing and decoration.

Architects like Sir Gilbert Scott (1811-78), Benjamin Ferrey (1810-80) and G.E. Street (1824-81) quickly found their feet in Gothic revival architecture. Scott's St Giles at Camberwell (London), begun in 1842, with its high chancel separated from the nave by the central tower, and geometrical tracery, shows him to have absorbed the writings of Pugin. He was a prolific architect, mainly in the Decorated style, who developed a preference for asymmetrical spires, and whose masterpiece was probably at Haley Hill, Halifax (West Yorkshire), of 1855-9. Ferrey built competently on a large scale, as at St Stephen Westminster of 1847-9, and on a small scale, as witnessed by his estate church at Merthyr Mawr (Glamorgan) of 1849-51. Street's Par church (Cornwall) of 1847 was much praised for its rugged simplicity, considered ideal for rural churches. *The Ecclesiologist* published articles extolling the qualities of Italian architecture, and Italian and Lombardic forms were part of a revived interest in Romanesque architecture. Wilton (Wiltshire), by Wyatt and Brandon of 1840-6, follows the early Christian basilican plan. Its exterior features an asymmetrical Italianate bell tower, or *campanile*. Meanwhile its interior incorporates architectural fragments salvaged from Italy, one of the many fruits of antiquarian tourism that found their way into British churches.

58 Bodelwyddan (Denbighshire), by John Gibson of 1856–60, is an exceptionally
well-detailed Decorated-style church with a fine tall spire

One of the most favoured characteristics of Italian Gothic was poly-chromy, advocated in the writings of John Ruskin and in the architecture of William Butterfield (1814-1900). His All Saints church in Margaret Street, Westminster (1849-59) was conceived as the model church of The Ecclesiological Society. Set back from the street, its only townscape impact is the tall spire. Its real contribution to the High-Victorian style is its decorative treatment. Built of brick, its exterior features diaper patterns in black brick, familiar from Tudor buildings, and Bath stone dressings. The interior is more richly treated with red, black and white bricks, green, yellow and grey glazed tiles. It differed from Pugin's Cheadle in that Pugin had his decoration painted on to plastered walls, whereas for Butterfield it was the wall itself that was coloured. Geometrical patterns have Venetian prototypes; the vaulted chancel ceiling owes something to the church of San Francesco, Assisi. Arcade piers are of polished red granite with alabaster capitals. This polychrome splendour was applied to his rural churches at Babbacombe (Devon) of 1865-74 and Penarth (Glamorgan) of 1865-6. Polychromy was also a feature of his furnish-ings and fittings, which include the rich font made for Ottery St Mary (Devon) that Butterfield restored.

Architects of High-Victorian churches were prolific and many had national reputations. S.S. Teulon (1812-73) built his best churches in London; William White (1825-1900) set up practice in Truro but also built in London, notably at St Saviour, Aberdeen Park, of 1865, as well as Lyndhurst (Hampshire) of 1858-69; John Loughborough Pearson (1817-97) was prolific across a wide area of England and Wales, with especially notable churches in the East Riding at Scorborough of 1857-9 and South Dalton of 1858-61, although his *magnum opus* is Truro Cathedral (1880-1910) (56). Other architects had more regional reputations. John Prichard (1817-86) was a pupil of Pugin and as Llandaf diocesan architect found plenty of work in South Wales. His masterpiece at Baglan (Glamorgan) of 1875-82 has a spire soaring above the surrounding suburban medioc-rity. The work of John Norton (1823-1904) of Bristol can be seen at its best at West Quantoxhead (Somerset) and at Beulah (Powys) of 1867.

There were further developments in architectural style in the final quarter of the nineteenth century. Self-consciously English churches were designed by G.F. Bodley (1827-1907), in partnership with Thomas Garner (1839-1906). Clumber Park (Nottinghamshire) of 1886-9 has a spire based on Patrington in the East Riding, and Hoar Cross

59 Hoar Cross (Staffordshire), by Bodley and Garner, was built 1872-6 in a self-
consciously English Gothic style. The tower is based on Ilminster, one of the finest
late Gothic Somerset towers

(Staffordshire) of 1872-6 has a tower based on Ilminster in Somerset (59). Hoar Cross is an egregiously large church for a rural setting, built in memory of Hugo Francis Meynell Ingram. It shows what an architect could achieve if a wealthy patron allowed him scope to develop his ideas in full. At Hoar Cross the chancel is higher than the nave, and is much more richly decorated both outside and in, emphasising in architecture the importance of the sacraments. The interior is dark – too dark to read a hymn book – but the vaulted chancel is brightly lit by large windows, glimpsed through a fine rood screen. The interior, therefore, is an idealisation of the medieval principle of the heavenly Jerusalem, but practical it is not.

William Burges (1827-81) was another architect who needed a wealthy patron to allow adequate expression of his ideas. Burges stands out from his contemporaries as an architect who concentrated on quality rather than quantity, and he differed from most of his profession in that he held no deep religious conviction. His devotion to Gothic was romantic and aesthetic. His secular works, in particular his work at Cardiff Castle and nearby Castell Coch for the Marquis of Bute, are rightly as celebrated as his churches. Churches designed and built by Burges number in single figures but they include Skelton and Studley Royal (North Yorkshire), built in the period 1871-8, which are outstanding works of their time. Both are in a powerful early French Gothic style, and have interiors of controlled opulence and a meticulous attention to detail.

Toward the end of the nineteenth century emerged the influence of Norman Shaw (1831-1912), pioneer of the Domestic Revival style, and of the Arts and Crafts movement. Shaw built some fine churches of his own, like Richards Castle in Shropshire (1890-3), but a better exponent was arguably the prolific Chester architect John Douglas (1829-1911). Douglas was busy on domestic and ecclesiastical commissions across Cheshire and north-east Wales, although his masterpiece is Hopwas (Staffordshire) of 1881. Typical of its architect, it incorporates brick with timber framing to give a domestic character, and has the chancel higher than the nave to give the kind of unexpected picturesque effect that he also employed elsewhere.

The Victorian period was also a great age of church restoration. Restoration is the most controversial aspect of Victorian architecture, although current opinion is perhaps less damning than it used to be. Nevertheless, restoration was usually a necessity not a luxury and churches that exhibit no nineteenth-century work are a small minority. By the early nineteenth century the nation's stock of medieval churches was largely in a poor state of repair. Liturgical changes over the Protestant centuries had left churches with many fixtures and fittings that needed replacing. Chief among these were the galleries that had been inserted into older churches. Ideal for auditory churches, they were impractical for a new liturgy that required the congregation to advance to the sanctuary to celebrate communion. Restoration was in most cases a necessity, although it was often done poorly. In their over-enthusiasm architects sometimes corrected the original building, ending up with a church that in a sense was more medieval than the Middle Ages. Sir Gilbert Scott, one of the busiest church restorers, wrote *A Plea for the Faithful Restoration of our Ancient Churches* (1850) in response to many ill-judged reinventions of the past. His own work could be very good, like the painstaking reconstruction of the Perpendicular tower of Taunton St Mary. In his *Seven Lamps of Architecture* (1849) John Ruskin (1819-1900) even questioned the whole notion that a building can be restored. It was in response to inept restoration that the Society for the Protection of Ancient Buildings was founded in 1877. Scraping the plaster from the walls was the worst mistake of Victorian restorers, not least because it removed many layers of history from the church. In medieval churches it produces a gloomy and untidy interior effect that is completely unhistorical. Another bane of Victorian intervention is not the fault of architects. Piecemeal acquisition of stained glass has led to haphazard collections of windows that filled their donors with pride but have done nothing for the lightness and visual coherence of the interior.

Not all Victorian restoration was bad, and nor is it always easy to identify. Medieval window tracery, for example, rarely survives in its original form, but in looking at a window it can be difficult to distinguish whether the tracery design is of the fifteenth or nineteenth century. Similarly the parapets of towers cannot be examined closely, and nor can medieval wooden roofs. External stone carving is prone to weathering, especially the softer limestones, and when an unrestored denuded moulding is compared with a restored example, it is evident that restoration is sometimes better than the original. Roofs were carefully rebuilt, often incorporating some of the original timber that had not succumbed to decay, but from ground level it is difficult to distinguish what belongs to which period and renders terms like 'medieval roof' ambiguous.

THE TWENTIETH CENTURY

In the first part of the twentieth century new churches continued to be built in the medieval Gothic style. Its chief exponents included Sir Ninian Comper (1864-1960), whose chief work, Wellingborough St Mary, looks back to the nineteenth century. The work of A.D. Caroe and A.P. Robinson, for example at Mile Cross, Norwich (Norfolk), similarly looks back. The Arts and Crafts movement was still strong before 1914, and includes Roker Park (Durham) of 1906-7 by E.S. Prior (1852-1932), where the transverse arches and simple tracery look forward to the simple, strong detail of concrete modernist architecture. The firm of Welch, Cachemaille-Day and Lander built two important churches near Manchester, at Burnage and Northenden, in the 1930s.

To its credit, the Church of England has not been afraid to embrace Modernist and post modern architecture. New cathedrals at Guildford (1961), Coventry (1962) and the Roman Catholic cathedral at Liverpool (1967) helped to stimulate interest in new church designs. Harringay St Paul (London) by Peter Jenkins, which opened in 1993, has many champions for its contemplative interior made of white-painted brick and black-painted wood.

5

THE EXTERIOR

Visit a number of churches around the country and it soon becomes apparent that the character of a building is largely defined by the materials with which it is built. Building materials are a major factor in the variety of parish churches, and one of the main reasons why we like them. Availability of building materials accounts for most things, from the style of towers to the scale and height of the remainder of the church.

A common source of early building materials was the masonry and bricks of ruined Roman buildings. Canterbury's Roman ruins were extensively exploited for building materials. Brixworth (Northamptonshire) has Roman bricks in its lower courses that were probably taken 24 miles from Leicester. In the north of England Roman buildings provided material not just for building walls, but also to provide ready-made architectural features: Roman arches can be seen re-assembled at Escomb (County Durham) and Corbridge (Northumberland) (see *19*). At Wroxeter (Shropshire), many fragments of masonry from the neighbouring Roman city were re-used, including a column base re-used as the font. Two masonry columns span the churchyard gate.

The best building stones, known as freestone, are capable of being finely carved and are best laid in regular courses. Limestones and sandstones fall into this category, although the quality can still be variable according to the fineness of grain and resistance to weather. The limestone band extending from Dorset, Somerset, the Cotswolds and up to Yorkshire provides the best stones. Churches in these districts are therefore the most ornately treated. In the late Middle Ages this meant an embattled parapet for the tower, nave, aisles and chancel (see *42*). The least desirable building stones are flint and chert that cannot be cut into regular-shaped blocks, let alone allow carving. Nor are these stones strong

60 Hales (Norfolk) is a twelfth-century flint church, to which a relatively plain round tower was added soon after. Nearly all round towers are in East Anglia, and Hales is fortunate to retain a traditional thatch roof

when they are bonded together to form a wall. Ironically, some of the nation's finest churches are found in these districts (*60*). In East Anglia, where flint was the main building material, the combination of flint and freestone was used to create a checkerboard pattern known as flushwork. Southwold, Eye and Long Melford (all Suffolk) are outstanding among many fine examples. In areas where the building stone is unyielding, such as Cornwall and west Wales, the churches have a plainer, more rugged external character (*61*).

Timber framing was an important building style in secular architecture of the sixteenth and seventeenth centuries, especially as it was easier to carve than stone and therefore offered greater opportunities for external display. There are a few late medieval timber-framed churches, such as Melverly (Shropshire) and Trelystan (Powys), but more often it was used only for parts of the building, perhaps the porch, of which there are many examples, or the tower, like Upleadon (Gloucestershire) (*62*). Greensted (Essex) belongs to a much earlier tradition of timber building. The split-log walls of its nave have been dated to the late eleventh century, making it the oldest timber church in Britain. Also of significance

Above: 61 Bosherston (Pembrokeshire)
has work from the thirteenth to the
nineteenth century, but is characterised
by its severe and tapering early
Perpendicular tower

Right: 62 Upleadon (Gloucestershire)
has a rare timber-framed tower, probably
of the sixteenth century

is that Greensted has a sixteenth-century chancel of brick. Brick made its first appearance in church architecture in this period, just as it did in secular architecture. Its use was confined to areas where the building stone was poor, such as Essex, which has other churches partly of brick, at Sandon and Fryerning.

Alongside new styles of church building in the eighteenth century came new building materials. Brick was established as a material suitable for polite architecture in the eighteenth century. Ironwork also became a more prominent material. Advances in foundry technology in the early eighteenth century made it easier to cast intricate items, while the greatly increased output of the iron industry put much more of the material on to the market. Cast iron was a convenient prefabricated material that could be cast to classical or Gothic forms as required. It found favour in the use of columns to support galleries, parallel to its adoption in nonconformist chapels. It was also a suitable material for windows, replacing wooden and lead glazing bars and stone mullions. The London firm of Underwood, Bottomley and Hamble supplied 'patent metal' sash windows to churches in the 1790s and published a catalogue in 1793 that included Gothic windows for chapels. Shrewsbury St Alkmund has intricately patterned iron windows, seemingly a one-off by the Coalbrookdale Company. (Further development of structural ironwork can be found inside churches – Thomas Rickman's St George Everton in Liverpool of 1812 boasts cast and wrought iron arcades, roof trusses and window tracery.)

The availability of building materials was to increase throughout the nineteenth century and beyond, the distribution of which was aided by the growth of the railway network. Bricks, roof tiles and stone, like Bath stone that was favoured for window dressings, all served a wide market and were one factor in the decline of local building styles. They were also used on the restoration of older churches, resulting in further dilution of the existing regional character. This was especially the case with roofing material. Thin North Wales slates (not the thicker traditional kind) and tiles became much cheaper than traditional building materials like thatch, and were in plentiful supply, in contrast to other traditional larger stone tiles that had been used in many regions.

Other external features are worthy of attention in their own right and are consistent across many architectural styles. When a church was completed it was formally dedicated and consecrated by carving 12 crosses on the exterior of the building. Susceptible to erosion, few such medieval crosses are now visible, although Edington (Wiltshire) retains 10 of them.

GARGOYLES AND HUNKY PUNKS

Gargoyles and hunky punks are the carvings found at the eaves level of the building, especially on towers. In the fifteenth century, when parapets were increasingly used as an aesthetically satisfying way of crowning a wall, disguising the visually awkward junction between wall and roof, water could no longer drain easily off the roof. Gargoyles are long projecting gutter stones, sometimes with additional lead spouts, that threw water off the roof away from the walls. The subject matter is usually a grotesque head or monster. Hunky punks, a term usually applied to the carvings on late medieval Somerset churches, are the grotesque carvings at eaves level that, unlike gargoyles, are purely decorative. Grotesque heads, monsters, monkeys and musicians all feature. These carvings are not confined to Somerset, but they do only appear on Gothic style churches. Gothic Revival architects provided them in abundance.

BELLCOTES

Ringing of bells was a familiar sound in the Middle Ages. The Angelus bell was rung three times daily to commemorate the Incarnation. Bells were also rung to call the faithful to Mass, and to mark baptisms and funerals. Not every church had the resources to provide a bell tower. Instead the bell or bells were housed in a small bellcote, usually at the west end, or were housed in the west wall of the church.

Peals of five or six bells, used for changing ringing, are a post-Reformation development from the seventeenth century onwards. Nevertheless Gothic Revival architects designed bellcotes or spirelets for small churches where a bell tower was not viable on aesthetic or financial grounds. Sir Gilbert Scott's spirelet at Chantry (Somerset) is typical of the care devoted to these structures that had an important aesthetic role in crowning the elevation of the building. Likewise the eastern gables of Victorian churches usually had a sculpted cross at the apex.

SUNDIALS

Sundials were used to mark time. In medieval churches sundials were almost invariably built on to the south wall of the nave or porch. These simple devices depend upon the shadow cast by a gnomon on to a dial with scratched markings. Anglo-Saxon sundials are known as tide dials because they divided the daylight hours into four sections, or tides. Kirkdale (North Yorkshire) has an example of $c.1055$, well preserved by the porch later built over it. Medieval dials are also known for obvious reasons as Mass dials. There is a good series of these dials around Cirencester (Gloucestershire), including Ampney Crucis, Coln St Aldwyns and Eastleach Turville. Sundials with hourly divisions belong after the Reformation. On medieval churches they were sometimes scratched on to existing masonry or, alternatively, comprise a square face of split stone with metal gnomon. Sundials were also erected in churchyards, and are described below.

CLOCKS

Clocks were a medieval invention – the late fourteenth-century clock at Wells Cathedral is the oldest working example – but few of them were installed at medieval parish churches. Wren incorporated clocks into his London churches, and clocks feature in James Gibbs' London churches of St Mary le Strand (1716) and St Martin-in-the-Fields (1726). However, most church clocks belong to the late nineteenth century and often are inscribed with the maker's name. These are testament to the once thriving local industry of clock making.

THE PORCH

Embellishment of the porch and the existence of both north and south porches in many churches are testament to the importance of a structure that initially served to protect the entrance of the church from the elements. In the medieval period the porch became a kind of liturgical ante-chamber where the first part of marriage and baptismal ceremonies took place. It was also used for the 'churching' of women, the ceremony that marked the end of a woman's confinement, and an important rite of passage representing the sanctity of childbirth.

Porches have also had many secular functions, acting as parish meeting rooms, school rooms and lock-ups. In the nineteenth century some housed fire engines and hearses. Increasing importance of secular functions during the Middle Ages is represented by the occasional addition of a second storey, used as a library, strong room, school room, and occasionally for domestic accommodation. Two-storey porches were a feature of late medieval parish churches. The upper storey was reached usually by means of a winding stone stair. The three-storey porch at Cirencester is the grandest of them all, although it was built as an administrative centre for an Augustinian Priory (63). Its entrance has iron gates, a feature that would become more popular in post-Reformation churches, and especially in the nineteenth century.

The interior of the porch might have stone or wooden benches in the side walls. They also have elaborate roofs similar to the nave roofs and, along with the lower stage of the tower which had a similar function, are the most likely place in a parish church to find stone vaulting.

63 The porch at Cirencester (Gloucestershire) was built in 1490 and is by far the largest of its date in Britain. It was built by the monastic landlords of the parish in order to conduct their secular business. It was also used for meetings of trade guilds and after the Reformation was for a time the town hall

Such elaboration expresses the building's importance. In the porch there would be a stoup on the right-hand side of the doorway into the main body of the church, comprising an arched recess for holy water. (If a church did not have a porch, stoups were also built into the external or internal nave walls.) It allowed worshippers to cross themselves with holy water on entering the church, a sign of popular devotion of the later medieval period. Above the door was a statue niche, similar to the niches on the outside of the porch, although if it is now filled with a statue of the patron saint it is probably a nineteenth-century replacement.

Porches were especially favoured by Gothic revival architects as an integral component of the parish church, providing an opportunity for external display of sculpture, and of similar sculpture over the main nave doorway. Porches of this period also had east and west windows with stained glass.

DOORS

Before entering a church it is always as well to have a good look at the door. Many churches retain medieval doors, often of a double thickness of planks held together by iron studs. Occasionally the original locks are still in use. One of the rare occasions when a locked church is a bonus is when you get hold of the original key and have a chance to appreciate the craftsmanship of the locksmiths. Decoration of doors is usually confined to ironwork. This was usually in the form of a long strap hinge that served the additional purpose of binding together the wooden battens. Norman work at Stillingfleet (North Yorkshire), Worfield (Shropshire) and at Staplehurst (Kent) comprises long strap hinges with large C-shaped scrolls and a pictorial scheme of simple profile shapes. Stillingfleet has a ship and Adam and Eve; Staplehurst has fish, a boat and zoomorphic motifs. In Gothic churches the hinge usually sprouts foliage. Thomas of Leighton provided ironwork for doors in the mid-thirteenth century at Leighton Buzzard, Eaton Bray and Turvey (all in Bedfordshire). The door at Dartmouth (Devon) is exceptional (64). It uses heraldic leopards for hinges and incorporates a tree sprouting branches to cover the entire surface of the door. Medieval smiths were also capable of manufacturing intricate door handles and lock plates. Wooden doors sometimes feature blind arcading and heraldic decoration. At Gedney (Lincolnshire) the fourteenth-century door bears a Latin inscription (65).

Right: 64 The magnificent fifteenth-century door at Dartmouth (Devon) has hinges of heraldic lions – the arms of the Plantagenet kings – bisected by a tree, probably representing the Tree of Life and covering and strengthening the entire area of the door

Below: 65 The fourteenth-century door at Gedney (Lincolnshire) has blind tracery or panels and bears a Latin inscription 'Pax Christi sit huic domui et omnibus habitantibus in ea hic requies nostra'

66 Studley Royal (North Yorkshire) by William Burges was completed in 1878 and is notable for its lavish details, including the ironwork of the west door. The long strap hinges bisected by C-scrolls recall Norman ironwork, while the tree expresses the fecundity of nature, a favourite Burges theme

Gothic revival architects also used strap hinges, although in some cases by opening the door it becomes apparent that they are fakes, and are sometimes of cast iron. William Burges designed elaborate hinges for his churches at Studley Royal and Skelton (North Yorkshire) and Lowfield Heath (Sussex) (66).

6

THE INTERIOR

WALL PAINTING

The interior walls of medieval churches were plastered and painted. In a few cases the paintings were applied to wet plaster and can properly be termed frescoes – Kempley (Gloucestershire), Coombes, Clayton and West Chiltington (all in Sussex) are surviving examples. The technique, however, was not as well suited to the damp climate of Britain as it was to Italy. In Britain the painting was more usually applied to dry plaster. Only simple pigments were used – lime for white, ochre for various shades of red and yellow, and charcoal for black. Much less common colours were blue derived from azurite or green derived from copper salt.

Medieval wall painting served three purposes: decoration, devotion and teaching. Figure painting was mainly for devotional purposes, at least in the early medieval period. The grandest schemes are to be found in the chancel rather than the nave (67). For decoration, the drawing of patterned lines in imitation of masonry was known as stoning. Alternatively or in combination with stoning, stencilled patterns of fleur-de-lis or rosettes could be used to cover wall surfaces (68).

Biblical scenes, including the lives of Christ and the Virgin Mary, were popular subjects. Narrative schemes of the life of Christ or the saints would be presented in a cartoon-strip fashion (69). For the battle between virtues and vices a more ingenious solution was found in the form of a long line of horsemen in combat with the vices, as can be seen at Claverley (Shropshire) and in repainted form at Copford (Essex) (70). Diagrammatical representation also found favour, like the wheel of virtue and vice at Kempley.

Above: 67 Twelfth-century figures of Apostles on the chancel wall at Kempley (Gloucestershire)

Left: 68 A twelfth-century wall painting at Coombes (Sussex) shows a figure supporting an arch, the underside of which is decorated with a stencilled pattern

Right: 69 Wall paintings at West Chiltington (Sussex) include the Passion cycle. These two scenes show Christ carrying the cross and the crucifixion

Below: 70 The struggle between virtue and vice is represented at Claverley (Shropshire) as a series of armed knights in combat

Apostles and Saints Catherine, George, Margaret were all popular in the late Middle Ages. Christopher, however, is the saint most commonly found, usually directly opposite the entrance so that he was the first figure people saw when they entered the church. He is usually shown carrying the child Christ across a stream. As the patron saint of travellers it was thought that to invoke the saint would be a safeguard against accidental death. Other popular single scenes included moral warnings, like the Sabbath-breaker at Breage (Cornwall), or the demon Tutivillus eavesdropping at the shoulders of gossiping women at Peakirk (Cambridgeshire).

In the nave the principle painting was the Doom, or Last Judgement, painted above the chancel arch. In the centre Christ sits in judgement over the living and the dead. The dead are the naked figures rising out of their coffins. On the left side is the heavenly Jerusalem, and on the right side are the damned condemned to Hell. Doom paintings were intended to remind worshippers of the ultimate fate of all human kind. Lay worshippers saw it above the rood – the image of the crucifixion with Saints Mary and John – that was directly below it. Salisbury St Thomas has the most complete medieval Doom, largely because it was carefully repainted after it was discovered under layers of whitewash in 1881. Others, like

71 The twelfth-century Doom at Clayton (Sussex) shows Christ framed by a mandorla, with heaven on the left and hell on the right

Clayton (Sussex) of *c.*1100 are faded but it is still possible to pick the elements of the scheme that saw little change in over 400 years (71).

Wall paintings were whitewashed at the Reformation. Actual destruction of medieval paintings occurred later, and mostly during Victorian restoration or rebuilding. The fashion for scraping plaster off the walls to reveal the core rubble stonework destroyed many otherwise concealed paintings. Discovery of wall paintings also interested some restorers who could not resist the temptation to repaint. Wall paintings on dry plaster had a limited lifespan, and so their replacement or repainting was a regular occurrence even in the Middle Ages. Nineteenth-century and later restorers have continued that tradition, notably at the churches of Copford (Essex) and at Salisbury St Thomas mentioned above.

After the Reformation words replaced images. Paintings were replaced by the texts of the Creed, Lord's Prayer and Ten Commandments, although these were in due course replaced by texts painted on to wooden boards. In the seventeenth century a few churches had their plaster ceilings painted. Bromfield (Shropshire), of 1672 by Thomas Francis, and Muchelney (Somerset) both have naïve depictions of angels in heaven. At Passenham (Northamptonshire) the chancel rebuilt in 1626 has strong Catholic tendencies, including the murals of prophets and Apostles who stand, not under Gothic niches, but between classical pilasters with their heads framed by shells.

Passenham was an exceptional example that existed because of the individual taste of its patron, Sir Robert Banastre. Such was also the case in the eighteenth century, when there was a partial renewed interest in visual adornment of the church. Little Stanmore (Greater London) and Great Witley (Worcestershire) have plaster walls and ceilings that incorporate paintings as an integral component of the decorative scheme. Little Stanmore was a medieval church rebuilt in 1715 for James Brydges, Duke of Chandos, by John James. He commissioned foreign painters to help adorn the interior: French painter Louis Laguerre (1663-1721) for the ceilings, probably Francesco Sleter for the Evangelists and Virtues on the side walls, and Venetian artist Antonio Bellucci for the east and west murals depicting the Descent from the Cross and the Nativity. The Duke of Chandos also had a private chapel at his nearby house at Cannons, but when house and chapel were demolished after his death in 1744 there was an auction of its art treasures. Lord Foley bought the pictures and much else that had adorned the chapel, and moved them to his church at Great Witley (Worcestershire). The church had been built in 1735 but Foley commissioned James Gibbs to redesign the interior. He employed Italian craftsmen, who recreated as far as possible the interior of the chapel at Cannons, including a papier maché ceiling which, being lighter than plaster, was needed for the wide span of the nave. On the ceiling are paintings by Antonio Bellucci, chief of which is the Resurrection (*colour plate 12*). Another notable painted ceiling is in the Georgian church completed in 1763 at West Wycombe (Buckinghamshire). It depicts the Last Supper and was painted by Giovanni Borgnis.

In Victorian churches the interior is often faced in ashlar, a deliberate expression of the materials that is opposed to hiding the structure of the building behind plaster. Pugin, although he had been the first to advocate the honest use of materials, reintroduced the idea of painting plastered walls. Victorian wall painting has been underrated, overlooked in favour of medieval wall painting whose chief virtue is usually not its artistic quality but its age. Victorian painting should be much better known and appreciated. It was endorsed by the Ecclesiologists, the model church of which at All Saints, Margaret Street, London, has paintings in the chancel.

Highnam (Gloucestershire) has one of the most complete and carefully thought-out schemes of wall painting in an Anglican church. It was built in 1849-51 by Thomas Gambier Parry as a memorial to his wife, with Henry Woodyer as architect. Parry designed the frescoes himself over a decade later, using a spirit-based paint of his own invention that allowed Italian fresco techniques to be used in England (*72*). The scheme includes a traditional Doom painting which is more beautiful if less frightening than its medieval predecessors (*colour plate 13*). Of other churches by Woodyer, Hascombe (Surrey) has nave wall paintings on the theme of the Miraculous Draught of Fishes, and Greenham (Berkshire) has painted saints and Biblical scenes on the chancel walls added in 1890. At Garton-on-the-wolds (East Riding) walls of the medieval church were painted by Clayton and Bell with the restoration of the church in 1865. The work is in their favoured thirteenth-century style and has Old Testament themes in the nave, New Testament in the chancel.

Subject matter of these paintings often reflected the individual preoccupations of the patrons. William White's masterpiece at Lyndhurst (Hampshire), for example, has a painting in the chancel depicting the parable of wise and foolish virgins, by Lord Leighton. And painting was often used as one element in an integrated scheme, which is how Street used

72 On the north aisle wall at Highnam (Gloucestershire) are paintings depicting Christ's entry to Jerusalem, executed by Thomas Gambier Parry in the 1870s

painting at St James the Less in Westminster, and Bodley used it at St John, Tue Brook (Liverpool), in both cases above the chancel arch. In most cases, however, paintings and stained glass were intended to complement one another. Pontargothi (Carmarthenshire) has murals designed by Benjamin Bucknall and completed in 1878. They form a complete scheme of Biblical scenes and inscriptions enclosed by Gothic arches, which complement the stained glass by Clayton & Bell. The paintings are monochromatic red and white. Although nineteenth-century painters had a greater range of colours available to them they sometimes preferred to work in the red and cream of medieval wall painting. At Hornblotton (Somerset) Sir T.G. Jackson designed patterns and foliage applied in a technique known as *sgraffito*, whereby red plaster is scratched with a design to reveal white plaster beneath.

GLASS

Coloured glass had been used in England from at least the seventh century, when Benedict Biscop sent for glaziers from France to work on his monasteries at Monkwearmouth and Jarrow. Not every church window had stained glass in the early Middle Ages, however. Most parish church windows were originally left open, or were protected from the weather with oiled linen. The use of stained glass increased in the later medieval period, as greater resources were devoted to church decoration, and changing architectural style, especially Perpendicular window tracery, called for glass-painted figures as a logical part of the window design. In this period light inside the parish church was refracted through coloured glass that created a jewelled light, evoking the jewels embellishing the heavenly city of Jerusalem.

Stained glass is a general term that covers a range of techniques and developments over time. In the early Middle Ages glaziers produced coloured glass by adding metal oxides, known as pot metal, to the glass mix in its molten state. Oxides produced various shades of red, purple, green and yellow. These were fitted together using lead strips known as cames. Details, texture and shading were also painted on the glass using a dark pigment of copper or iron oxide, and were then fired in a kiln. Grisaille glass was a cheaper, simpler form of decorative glass. Clear glass was painted with black foliage or geometrical designs before firing. The best example in England is probably the window of c.1260 at York Minster. Grisaille was probably the most common form of glass in parish churches before the fifteenth century but little of it survives. Brabourne (Kent) has the earliest surviving grisaille panel in England, and other grisaille windows are at Stodmarsh (Kent).

Glass staining was discovered in the early fourteenth century (73). Silver nitrate was used to paint the glass, which was then fired in an oven to produce various shades of yellow. From the sixteenth century glass painting was introduced from Germany, from where many immigrant craftsmen were employed. Coloured enamel pigments, made up of finely ground glass, were painted on the glass and were made permanent by firing. Glass painting greatly reduced the importance of the lead cames.

The subject matter of medieval glass exhibits a range of sources similar to wall painting. The largest schemes were the important focal points of the east and west windows. Traditionally the east window would depict the Crucifixion, and its counterpart in the west window would be the Last Judgment. Fairford (Gloucestershire) retains fine examples of both (*colour plate 14*). Other episodes in the life of Christ were also popular, such the Nativity and Ascension (74). Scenes from the life of Christ fill

73 Eaton Bishop (Herefordshire) is a parish church with early fourteenth-century glass of high quality. This panel shows the Archangel Michael

the east window of St Peter Mancroft in Norwich. The genealogy of Christ, known as the Tree of Jesse, was a literal family tree that traced Christ's descent from Jesse the father of David. In medieval art Jesse is depicted as a reclining figure from which a trunk emanates that sprouts the branches bearing his descendants, and crowned by Mary with the infant Jesus. Shrewsbury St Mary (Shropshire) retains a fine example of *c.*1330 in the east window. The subject reached the height of its popularity in the fourteenth century, although enjoyed a revival of interest from the late fifteenth century, from which period are the Jesse windows at Leverington (Cambridgeshire), Margaretting (Essex) and at Llanrhaedr-yng-Nghinmeirch (Denbighshire), which is dated 1533.

74 Detail of a late fifteenth-century window at East Brent (Somerset) depicting the Ascension

The other popular subject matter for stained glass in medieval parish churches was the depiction of saints. Single figures of saints were well suited to the mullioned windows of the fourteenth to the sixteenth centuries. The most common form was to frame a single figure within an architectural canopy, and to elongate the figure to fit the space available. Saints can be identified by the accompanying object, or attribute. For example Mary Magdalene was depicted with the pot of ointment that she used to anoint Christ; Margaret and George are depicted as dragon slayers. The four Evangelists – Matthew, Mark, Luke and John had emblems respectively of an angel, winged lion, winged ox and eagle, derived from the winged beasts at God's throne described in the book of Revelation. Most saints' emblems depicted their method of martyrdom. Hence Catherine is shown with the wheel she was tied to, Laurence with a gridiron. Saints dominate the east window of the Beauchamp Chapel in Warwick St Mary, Richard Beauchamp's mid fifteenth-century chantry chapel. Its glass was made by John Prudde, the king's glazier, in 1447-50.

With the Reformation the demand for stained glass abruptly declined. Heraldic glass now became the most common subject, one that had been a minor subject matter in the medieval period. Stained glass enjoyed a mini revival in the eighteenth century when glass painters developed enamel paints that produced an effect similar to oil paintings. In fact oil paintings were often the direct inspiration for windows. William Peckitt (1731 95) continued the long tradition of stained glass makers in York. His work can be seen at St Anne, the Georgian church in central Manchester, and in a depiction of the Last Supper at Audley End (Essex). Francis Eginton of Birmingham produced theatrical Biblical images, such as his version of the Assumption of the Virgin Mary, based upon an oil painting by Guido Reni, at Shrewsbury St Alkmund (Shropshire) (colour plate 15)

Most parish church glass belongs to the nineteenth century, when glaziers busied themselves meeting the demands imposed by new buildings and the restoration of medieval churches. Interest in the techniques of medieval glass preceded the influence of Pugin, whose stimulus did as much for the revival of stained glass as it did for all things medieval. Early pioneers of medieval-style glass included Thomas Willement, and John Hardman of Birmingham, one of Pugin's collaborators (75).

Left: 75 The east window of Tenbury Wells (Worcestershire) is by Hardman of Birmingham and depicts the Transfiguration of Christ

Opposite: 76 South Dalton (East Riding) east window, by Clayton & Bell, depicts the Day of Judgment. St Michael weighs souls in the centre. The saved are on the left and on the right are the damned, who proceed in orderly fashion to Hell, quite unlike the horror of the medieval version

Firms such as Clayton & Bell soon established a reputation as high-quality glass painters, having studied and reproduced the styles of the early medieval period, mainly with reds and blues (*76*). More painterly effects were produced by glaziers influenced by the later medieval period, which offered a greater repertoire of colours. Charles Kempe (1837-1907) began his career in the office of the architect George Bodley, but he subsequently became a prolific stained-glass artist, notably producing work for Bodley and Garner's Hoar Cross (Staffordshire). Other stained-glass makers worthy of note include the large firm of Powell & Sons of Whitefriars, London (for whom Edward Burne-Jones was erstwhile chief designer but who generally produced unexciting glass), Heaton, Butler & Bayne, and Morris, Marshall, Faulkner & Co. (later known as Morris & Co.). The latter firm was founded by William Morris as a reaction against the mass-

production of glass, and developed new colour tones and a style more integrated with the architecture of the building. Selsley (Gloucestershire) was their first commission, a church by Bodley built in 1862. It features designs by William Morris, Ford Maddox Brown, Edward Burne Jones and Philip Webb. Its picture windows form a continuous band, above and below which is lighter grisaille glass to emit light (*colour plate 16*).

A fair proportion of Victorian and later stained glass is signed. Glaziers adopted their own special marks, often as simple as a monogram, which can usually be found in one of the bottom corners of a window. Charles Kempe's wheatsheaf makes his work easy to identify (although a practised eye will soon be able to identify his glass from the distinctive painterly effect), as is the friar's habit adopted by Powell & Sons of Whitefriars.

Whereas the style of Victorian glass has been much studied, less attention has been paid to the content of the windows. In some fortunate churches the glass in all the windows follows a consistent theme. Usually, however, the stained glass is more varied and was installed piecemeal as an act of commemoration. Saints remained important, although without the same devotional connotations that they had in medieval churches. Crucifixion and Resurrection are also well represented and remained the most appropriate scene for an east window. Other narrative scenes from the New Testament displayed the Biblical knowledge of the glass painters and their patrons. Popular scenes include the presentation of the infant Jesus at the Temple, Jesus attending Jairus's daughter (not dead but sleeping), Christ on the Sea of Galilee and the parable of the Good Samaritan. Some of them, like numerous windows on the theme of Christ saying 'Suffer little children to come unto me', cross the line into sentimentality. Edward Burne Jones, who later in his career was chief designer for Morris & Co., introduced a new motif of Christ holding a lantern, a metaphor of Christ as the light of the world.

Later nineteenth-century stained-glass artists were influenced by the Pre-Raphaelites and the Arts and Crafts movements, as in the work of Christopher Whall and Henry Holiday. In the work of some Scots glaziers, like William Wilson and Douglas Strachan, the Arts and Crafts tradition thrived well into the twentieth century (77).

77 The life of St Edith of Wilton (961-84) is shown in a window at her birthplace of Kemsing (Kent), by Douglas Strachan, of 1935. Edith was the illegitimate daughter of Edgar, king of England

The traditional Victorian-medieval style also continued to thrive in the prolific output of Powells and other firms. A post-war revival in stained glass was stimulated by work for the new Coventry Cathedral. John Piper, in collaboration with Patrick Reyntiens, made both abstract and figurative windows. Other regional glass makers have also thrived, such as the Swansea firm of Celtic Studios, who have produced modernist-figurative designs since 1948. In exceptional circumstances artists have been able to design a complete scheme of glass for an entire church, like the remarkable commemorative and abstract windows at Tudeley (Kent), designed by Marc Chagall (1887-1965) and installed over the period 1967-78 (*colour plate 17*).

ROOD SCREENS, CHANCEL SCREENS AND PARCLOSE SCREENS

Screens were used to close off separate sections within the church. In a medieval church a rood screen divided nave from chancel and parclose screens divided the nave and aisles from private parts of the church such as chantry chapels. Neither was essential, but offered an opportunity for wealthy parishes and individual benefactors to adorn their churches.

The rood screen had practical as well as symbolic functions. In a period when farm animals were sometimes brought into the church it was an effective barrier between secular and sacred parts of the church. The loft was used at Easter to perform Passion plays, and was bedecked with candles and flowers. The symbolic function of the screen was that it framed the performance of the Mass for the benefit of the lay worshippers. In this context it has to be imagined with the images of saints on the dado, the crucifixion above it, all superimposed by the Doom painting. The eastern bay of the roof above the screen was often more richly treated than the remainder, with a ceilure painted to represent a starry firmament. By looking east, much of the Christian doctrine could be read into screen, rood and Doom. Parclose screens were similar in design to rood screens, but without the necessity of a loft.

Rood screens are named after an Old English word for cross, because above and separate from the screen was a beam supporting an image of the crucifixion, St Mary and John the Baptist. Breamore (Hampshire) retains an Anglo-Saxon rood that was repositioned over the south doorway as early as the twelfth century. Rood screens became more prominent in the later medieval period, and express the popular piety and material prosperity of the later Middle Ages. Although comparatively few have survived, their former presence is marked by the winding stone stair, usually on the south side in the nave wall, that gave access to the loft. Some of the earliest surviving rood screens are built of stone, like the fourteenth-century screens at Stebbing and Great Bardfield (Essex), both designed like large traceried windows. Most screens are of wood and display all the skill and intricacy of medieval craftsmanship. They were constructed with a dado of blank panels, often painted, above which the screen was open between mullions and tracery, the latter often intricately carved with subsidiary tracery bars. Over the top of the screen was a loft supported on a deeply projecting coving, often resembling stone vaulting in its form, and then finished by a cornice (tiers of ornate friezes) crowned with an ornate crest known as brattishing.

Surviving screens are concentrated in three main regional groups: the England–Wales border region of Powys, Herefordshire and Shropshire; Devon, Cornwall and west Somerset; and East Anglia. There are plenty of exceptions, however, like the fine restored screen at Flamborough (East Riding).

The style in each of the main regions differs. The screen at Llananno (Powys) was salvaged when the old church was entirely rebuilt in 1876–77. It features the intricate tracery characteristic of the Mid Wales school of carvers, of which it is the best surviving example (78). The loft front has 25 canopied niches for saints, all removed at the Reformation, but with new figures inserted in 1880. The structure of screens in Wales, where other fine examples can be seen at Bettws Newydd, Llangwm Uchaf (both Monmouthshire) and Partrishow (Powys), is similar to those of the English border counties. St Margarets and Aymestry (both Herefordshire) and Hughley (Shropshire) are each masterpieces of craftsmanship with their simple, strong designs with deep panelled coving, in which intricate carving is subordinate to the main structural members (79, colour plate 18).

The characteristic West Country rood screen has coving resembling fan vaulting, and cornices incorporating tiers of vine trails (80). There are many fine examples, including Atherington, Bovey Tracy, Kenton, Cullompton, Plymtree (all Devon), Carhampton and Dunster (Somerset). The dado was sometimes carved in a similar manner to bench ends, with low-relief ornamentation, or simple pictorial representations such as heraldic devices or Passion symbols, as at St Buryan and St Levan (Cornwall). Otherwise it had painted images of saints,

78 Llananno (Powys) has the finest of the surviving rood screens of Mid-Wales. It has intricately carved coving and loft, with figures reinstated in the nineteenth century

79 The sixteenth-century rood loft at St Margarets (Herefordshire) is attached to the chancel wall, without the need of a screen

as in numerous Devon examples. In Norfolk the screens are larger but comparatively fewer of its lofts have survived. Many screens retain traces of their original figures, like the saints on the screens at Barton Turf, Ranworth, Ludham and Castle Acre (all Norfolk), which were painted on to the dado (*colour plate 19*). Attleborough (Norfolk) screen of *c.*1500 also has faded figures of saints, and on the loft the arms of all the English Episcopal sees.

At the Reformation the images associated with rood screens were removed. The rood was taken down, whereas painted screens were white-washed and the images were replaced with text, as at Binham Priory (Norfolk) (see 7). In many cases the rood and parclose screens themselves were retained as a useful means of detaching the chancel when it was considered of lesser importance.

Screens were also employed in post-Reformation churches. Post-Reformation screens adopted Renaissance motifs and the revival of classical forms. Now the uprights had fluted pilasters, arches were round not pointed, and the decoration was Renaissance inspired, including the relief patterning known as strapwork. Chancel screens were crowned not

80 The rood screen at Widecombe-in-the-Moor (Devon) is part restoration, but it retains its original painted dado and delicate carving

by a figure of the crucified Christ, but by the Royal Arms, symbolising the monarch as the head of the Church of England. Fine examples are at Croscombe (Somerset) dated 1616, Tilney All Saints (Norfolk) dated 1618 and Leeds St John (West Yorkshire) of 1632-4. Sir Christopher Wren had chancel screens built for Ingestre (Staffordshire) and the London churches St Peter Cornhill and All-Hallows-the-Great (now moved to St Margaret Lothbury) (*colour plate 9*).

Reinstatement of the rood screen occurred in the nineteenth-century Gothic revival. Pugin's screen at Cheadle (Staffordshire) has already been mentioned. Screens were now conceived as an integral component of the building, unlike medieval screens that were installed in churches already mostly more than a century old. G.F. Bodley built sumptuously detailed screens for churches such as Clumber Park (Nottinghamshire), Hoar Cross (Staffordshire) and St John, Tue Brook (Liverpool), which are modelled on the Devon type of medieval screen. Devon and Cornwall also have nineteenth-century rood screens, such as the fine example at Blisland (Cornwall) by F.C. Eden, of 1896. Most of these screens were of wood. James Brooks built a stone screen at St John in Holland Park (London) that integrates well with the stone-vaulted church. Some screens are of wood on stone foundations, such as William White's church at Lyndhurst (Hampshire). In many cases there is a stone base without a wooden superstructure, reference to the removal of screens at the Reformation. The Gothic style continued into the twentieth century in the work of Sir Ninian Comper and W.D. Caroe (*81*). Comper was a restorer as well as a maker of new screens, and his best screen is in his own church at Wellingborough St Mary (Northamptonshire).

Iron screens and gates had occasionally been used to partition chapels since the late medieval period, and enjoyed popularity in the late nineteenth century. Stanton Harcourt (Oxfordshire) has fine eighteenth-century iron gates leading to the chancel. At St John in Chester is a seventeenth-century chapel screen and gates of wood and iron. In the nineteenth century Butterfield used ironwork gates at All Saints, Margaret Street in Westminster (London), and elsewhere. Henry Wilson designed ironwork and other fittings for J.D. Sedding, and provided the iron fittings, including a fine Arts-and-Crafts screen at Norton-sub-Hamdon (Somerset). St Bees (Cumbria) has a late nineteenth-century ironwork screen filling the entire chancel arch.

81 The twentieth-century rood screen at Kemsing (Kent) is by W.F. Unsworth, with crucifixion, angels and Royal Arms by Sir Ninian Comper

ROYAL ARMS

Royal Arms symbolised the authority of the king and began to appear in parish churches after Henry VIII became Supreme Head of the Church of England in 1534. Many early examples were placed over the rood screen in place of the rood, but they were taken down with the accession of Mary. The practice of erecting Royal Arms was revived from the reign of Elizabeth onwards. Not until after the accession of Charles II in 1660 were churches obliged to display the Royal Arms, many examples of which had been destroyed during the Commonwealth.

Royal Arms are sometimes constructed of carved wood or plaster, but the majority are painted on boards. Some of them are placed above the chancel screen or chancel arch, and at Weston-under-Lizard (Staffordshire) on the altar rails (see *8, colour plate 9*). Most of them,

however, are fixed to the walls. Composition of the Arms underwent
many changes over time, for example with the accession of James VI
of Scotland to the English throne, and with the accession of the House
of Hanover. The majority of surviving Royal Arms are Georgian or
Victorian; very few belong to the twentieth century, but there are a fair
number belonging to the sixteenth and seventeenth centuries.

The main element of the Arms is a shield divided into quarters and
symbolising the three lions of England, red lion of Scotland, and the
Irish golden harp with silver strings (82). Until 1801 they also contained
gold fleur-de-lis symbolising the monarchs' claim to the French throne.
Around the shield is a belt or strap with the motto of the Order of the
Garter: 'Honi soit qui mal y pense' (evil to him who evil thinks). The
shield is crowned by a helmet and crest, and is held aloft by lion and
unicorn supporters, representing England and Scotland. They stand on
a 'compartment' that incorporates the sovereign's motto 'Dieu et mon
droit' (God and my right).

82 Royal Arms
of George III at
Widworthy (Devon)

CHANCEL AND CHAPELS

In early medieval churches the chancel was the most sumptuously fitted part of the church. Later in the medieval period the chancel was
less likely to be the most visually rich part of the interior, not from
any change in the liturgical requirements, but because it had been out-
done by lay investment in other parts of the church. The chancel did not
regain its status in visual and decorative terms until the Gothic revival of
the nineteenth century.

Chancel and chapels were for celebrating Mass and therefore required
altars, the central fixture around which architectural embellishment of
the chancel was constructed. Medieval altars were built of stone slabs.
They were consecrated by carving small crosses at the corners and in the
centre, symbolising the five wounds of Christ. Apart from the high altar,
and those in specially constructed chapels, side altars could also be found
in the nave, aisles, tower, porch (only rarely, as at Melton Mowbray in
Leicestershire) or the chamber above the porch. Very few have survived:
Arundel (Sussex) retains four altars, Peterchurch (Herefordshire) three.
Partrishow (Powys) also retains three altars, two of which are set up in
the nave against the rood screen. Tattershall (Lincolnshire) had two stone
altars recessed within the rood screen that were consecrated in 1528.
Ranworth (Norfolk) also had two altars set up against the screen.

Wooden canopies were commonly built above the high altar, although
few survived beyond the Reformation. These were set high to avoid
smoke blackening from altar candles, and so as not to obstruct the
view of the reredos, which is described below. Clun and Ludlow (both
Shropshire) retain panelled canopies. Michaelchurch (Herefordshire) has
an arched canopy much like a wagon roof. Likewise Gyffin (Gwynedd)
has an arched canopy spanning the full width of the chancel, and retains
its original painted figures.

The importance of the altar was expressed by the pictorial or sculpted
frame built behind it, known as the reredos or altar piece. This had
painted wooden panels or, if the structure was of stone, sculpted figures
in niches. Reredoses highlight the ritual importance of the altar and, for
that reason, suffered badly from Reformation and Puritan iconoclasm.
The greatest proportion of surviving medieval reredoses are in side chapels rather than the chancel, perhaps reflecting the greater prevalence of a
reredos for the minor altars – behind the high altar a large stained glass

window provided a suitable backdrop, the space below which would allow for only a small reredos. The mutilated frames of transept reredoses at Wells St Cuthbert (Somerset) are among the earliest and most impressive instances of the form in parish churches. At the Reformation their figures were removed and the niches plastered over, in which state they remained until nineteenth-century restoration. At the base of the south transept reredos is the low-relief figure of Jesse and low-relief foliage on the stone frame of what was once an impressive Tree of Jesse in stone. The earlier, thirteenth-century north transept reredos has a more straightforward arrangement of five statue niches which formerly had two tiers of figures. At Ranworth, mentioned above, the side altars have a reredos of painted panels incorporated into the rood screen. In the later Middle Ages the reredos more commonly became an architectural feature. Milton Abbey (Dorset), formerly monastic, has a large late fifteenth-century chancel reredos comprising three tiers of stone niches and Latin inscriptions. The restored reredos at Ludlow (Shropshire) is a similar architectural screen of sculpted images. A much better executed work is the fourteenth-century reredos at Llantwit Major (Glamorgan), comprising tiers of niches under canopies and arches, and extending across doorways to the sacristy.

For the celebration of Mass a basin was needed for washing the celebrant's hands and liturgical vessels, both of which carried residues of the Real Presence of Christ. Known as the piscina, the basin was usually built into the wall as an arched recess on the south side of the altar, with a drain to allow the water and wine to flow away into consecrated ground. Some Norman examples were pillar piscinas – such as at Kilpeck (Herefordshire), Wells St Cuthbert (Somerset) and Stanton Fitzwarren (Wiltshire) – which, as their name suggests, were freestanding structures on stone pedestals. From the late thirteenth century a fashion developed for double piscinas, supposedly providing one basin for the hands, the other for the vessels. A piscina was required for each altar in the church, not just in the chancel, and their survival is a sure indicator of the former presence of altars in aisles and transepts. Some piscinas had a higher shelf, or credence, on which the vessels for the Mass were placed before their consecration. Alternatively the credence could have been a wooden table or bracket. In exceptional circumstances a stone credence was built – at Stanford (Berkshire) the credence shelf is a polygonal stone niche above the piscina.

In the chancel the piscina was often linked compositionally with the three priests' seats known as the sedilia (plural of sedillum). Hedingham (Essex) is a Norman work of round arches on round columns. Acton Burnell (Shropshire) has a fine late thirteenth-century composition of piscina and sedilia framed by slender shafts, which are integrated with the overall design of the chancel that includes slender shafts and arches around the internal reveals of the windows (known as rere arches). Rushden (Northamptonshire), Swavesey (Cambridgeshire), Patrington (Yorkshire) and Adderbury (Oxfordshire) are all later Gothic chancels with integral piscina and sedilia. Enriched stone canopies framing sedilia and piscina are among the best-preserved works of architectural sculpture, having been protected from several centuries of weathering. The most ornate medieval examples belong to the fourteenth century. Heckington (Lincolnshire) is especially notable, part of its lavish chancel

83 Heckington (Lincolnshire) has elaborate sedilia of the 1330s, incorporating sculpted figures above the arches

sculpture created *c.*1330 and described again below (*83*). Its arches have fashionable S-curves (ogee arches) and gables, added to which are various figures amid foliage. A related slightly later work at Hawton (Nottinghamshire) is similar.

An aumbry, on the north side of the chancel, was a cupboard used for storage of the vessels used in the Mass and at baptism, and was usually a rectangular recess with wooden door. It did not rival the piscina in importance and so was never as richly treated. There are, however, aumbries in fine arched or gabled recesses, such as at Sefton (Lancashire). Vestments were stored in chests or, alternatively, these items could have been stored in a separate sacristy, although they were rare in medieval parish churches. Hemel Hempstead (Hertfordshire) has a Norman vaulted sacristy. At North Petherton (Somerset) the sacristy projects from the east end of the chancel and is as richly treated as the chancel itself, with embattled parapet.

One of the most significant architectural embellishments of the chancel was the fashion that emerged in the fourteenth century for building a Tomb of Christ (also known as an Easter Sepulchre). It was associated with the rituals of Holy Week, and of the feast of Corpus Christi, which had been proclaimed in 1317 by Pope John XXII to draw attention to the sanctity of the Eucharist and to the Real Presence of Christ in the consecrated host. In the succeeding decades Tombs of Christ became a common sight. The Tomb of Christ was usually a temporary construction of wood and canvas that was renewed every year. Of permanent structures the best examples are in the East Midlands, where many fourteenth-century churches built by wealthy benefactors have sculpted tombs in the north wall. They include Arnold, Hawton, Sibthorpe (all Nottinghamshire), Bottesford, Heckington, Irnham, Maxey and Navenby (all Lincolnshire) (*84, colour plate 20*). At Patrington (East Riding) the Tomb of Christ shows sleeping soldiers at the base, and Christ emerging from the tomb. Heckington of *c.*1330 is an outstanding work of architectural sculpture, bearing reliefs of sleeping soldiers and other figures (*84*). Hawton is of a similar design and 10 years later, and was built side-by-side with the tomb of its donor. It has sleeping soldiers at the base below canopied niches in which are damaged high-relief figures of Christ, the Virgin Mary and Mary Magdalene, above which is the Ascension. On Easter Sunday the consecrated host was laid in the breast of the Christ figure in the tomb.

Left: 84 The
Tomb of Christ
at Heckington
(Lincolnshire), of
*c.*1330, features the
empty tomb and,
beneath it, sleeping
soldiers in low relief

Opposite: 85 The
early eighteenth-
century altar rails
at Warkworth
(Northumberland)
are of wrought iron

After the Reformation the Eucharist was de-mystified – stone altars
were replaced by wooden communion tables, which were now brought
into the body of the church. Alternatively the chancel was opened up
and the communicants were allowed to sit at benches around the table.
The redundant church at Langley (Shropshire) retains this early seventeenth-century arrangement. Under the influence of Archbishop Laud,
archbishop of Canterbury from 1631, communion tables were set against
or close to the east wall. Altar rails had not been required before the
Reformation, since at that time the priests took the sacrament to the
celebrants in the nave. Since celebrants were now required to kneel
before the altar to receive the sacrament, altar rails served as a barrier to
kneel against and as a symbolic boundary that maintained the dignity
of the communion table. In practice most communion tables were not
railed until after the Restoration in 1660, or even as late as the eighteenth century.

Pre-Victorian altar rails usually extended right across the chancel,
but in some cases the rails form three sides of a rectangle against the
east wall of the chancel. Lyddington (Rutland) retains rails on four sides
of a communion table set well forward from the east wall. Early altar

rails resemble wooden balustrades with their turned balusters, much like the balustrading on contemporary secular staircases (see *105*). In the eighteenth century some altar rails were built in wrought iron, like at Warkworth (Northumberland) and Great Witley (Worcestershire) (*85*). At Weston-under-Lizard (Staffordshire) the iron altar rails are adorned with the Royal Arms of Queen Anne. Comparatively few churches retain altar rails earlier than 1850, since the chancel underwent significant re-design in the wake of the Anglican Revival.

Design and decoration of the chancel was revived in post-Reformation churches. In Anglican churches it was customary to fix a board with the Decalogue – the Ten Commandments, Creed and Lord's Prayer – behind the altar. From this developed the notion of assembling the boards in a formal altar piece, essentially a classical screen with pilasters and a pediment. This was less a symbolic necessity than an aesthetically satisfying way of treating the east end. Wren had several such altar pieces built for London churches, including the elaborate examples at St Stephen Walbrook and St Mary Abchurch. The altar piece at All Hallows-the-Great features flanking statues of Moses and Aaron. The classical-style reredos was occasionally used to fill the east wall of a medieval chancel in place of an east window, as at Bruton (Somerset). Elegant and under-stated, these ideas would be swept away by the Gothic revival in the nineteenth century.

In the nineteenth century the restoration of the chancel to its former importance was accompanied by new ideas about its decoration. Victorian architects divided the chancel into two compartments, the choir with its stalls set sideways, and the sanctuary behind the commun-ion rails. They also liked stepped chancels that elevated the altar at the east end. In order to house vestments and plate, vestries became com-mon, and were added to earlier churches. In many cases, however, these semi-utilitarian additions spoil the north view of the building. Likewise, the chancel came to accommodate the church choir, and in so doing it was deemed convenient to house the church organ in another projec-tion in the chancel wall.

The use of painted plaster, brick and masonry of various hues to line the chancel walls has already been described. One of the other principal means by which chancels were adorned was in the use of decorative tiles (*86*). Firms such as Minton of Stoke, Maw & Co. of Jackfield (Shropshire) and Godwin of Lugwardine (Herefordshire) produced decorative and glazed tiles in various colours. They were used for floors and for walls. Decorative tiles followed medieval prototypes, such as the use of sepa-rate clays to create a pattern of two colours – encaustic tiles. Tiles were laid in the central aisle, but richer treatment was usually given to the tiles laid on the sanctuary floor. Walls were also hung with tiles, often in conjunction with a reredos. At All Saints, Margaret Street, London, more ambitious ceramic murals were employed. Another opulent solution was to lay the floor with mosaic. For the chancel floor of Studley Royal (North Yorkshire) William Burges designed mosaic floors depicting in the choir the principal buildings of Jerusalem, and in the sanctuary the Garden of Eden with an angel guarding its gate.

Reredoses enjoyed a significant revival in the nineteenth century, and old and new churches alike needed them (*87*). Victorian designers had at their disposal a greater range of materials than their medieval predeces-sors – marble, freestone of various hues, mosaic, tiles and wood. In many cases they were installed in new churches some years after they were completed. Medieval churches were also furnished with reredoses, but in many cases they extend above the sill of the east window, obscuring a view of the glass. Victorian and later designers repeated the themes of

86 The chancel at Pugin's Cheadle (Staffordshire) revived the Tomb of Christ, and has a stepped floor to raise the altar above the remainder of the church. The decorative tiles are by Minton of Stoke

87 Hallow (Worcestershire) of 1867–9 has a Crucifixion reredos by Boulton of Cheltenham

their medieval predecessors, with influences from France and Italy as well as native sources. Comper took the Gothic tradition well into the twentieth century and maintained the tradition for opulent reredoses and altar canopies. His Wellingborough St Mary (Northamptonshire) features a baldacchino, a cloth canopy over the altar, on gilded Corinthian columns. A baldacchino is the most ambitious form of altar canopy, of which there are no ancient examples left in Britain.

7
FURNISHINGS

FONTS

The font was the earliest item of church furniture to be installed in the nave. Baptism was the rite that initiated infants into the Christian religion and, with the Eucharist, is one of only two Christian rites for which there is Biblical authority. Christ was baptised in the River Jordan and in early Christian communities adults were baptised by submersion in a special pool, a practice still maintained by the Baptist church. In medieval parish churches fonts were provided for infant baptism, which occurred preferably on the day of the child's birth. The Anglican church continued the rite of infant baptism in fonts although in the late nineteenth century there was a mini revival for building baptismal pools within the church. Llanbister (Powys) has a rare baptism pool, added by W.D. Caroe and H. Passmore in their restoration of the church in 1908.

The importance of baptism as a rite of passage is reflected in the care and attention devoted to fonts. Fonts in which a candidate underwent a symbolic cleansing are rich in symbolism. The longevity of fonts has given them an additional symbolic importance in the continuity of the faith over many centuries. Fonts do not decay quickly and were usually respected during later enlargement of churches, with the result that the font is often the oldest feature associated with the building and is a good indicator of when the parish church was founded. For these reasons fonts are among the most rewarding subjects of study in a parish church.

The great wave of church building that took place in the twelfth century was accompanied by the provision of countless finely decorated fonts, with the result that Norman fonts are more plentiful than Norman architecture. The Perpendicular style is also prevalent among fonts, part of the great rebuilding of parish churches in the later Middle Ages. In a medieval baptism the infant was immersed in the water, and so the diameter of the font basin had to be the length of an average newborn. The ceremony was performed using consecrated water that had been blessed for the occasion. The water remained in the font at all times and, to prevent the misappropriation of consecrated water for other uses, from the thirteenth century fonts were covered and locked. Font basins were lead-lined to prevent seepage through porous stone. Although most medieval font covers were at some stage discarded, evidence of the former fastenings can be seen around the rim of medieval fonts in the form of pairs of staple holes. Existence of holes and of lead lining is one of the indicators that a font is medieval, which is not always easy to tell.

After the Reformation the rite of baptism changed slightly, but its importance was undiminished. Infants were no longer immersed. Instead water was poured on to the child's head in a symbolic cleansing. For that reason the basins of post-Reformation fonts could be narrower. As holy water was not kept permanently in the font a cover was no longer essential, although often preferred for aesthetic reasons.

The earliest fonts are simple round stone tubs. If they have no decoration it is not possible to date them (the argument that plain fonts are more primitive and must therefore be Anglo-Saxon should be resisted). Deerhurst (Gloucestershire) has a font of probable Anglo-Saxon date, given the date of the church. It had been discarded from the church but was rescued from a farmyard in the nineteenth century, albeit in poor condition. The simple cylindrical tub is covered with a spiral decoration. This kind of abstract decoration is regularly found on Norman fonts, although more common is the use of arcading to frame and regularise the decoration. At Partrishow (Powys) is a tub font on a later pedestal, which can be dated to the mid-eleventh century by an inscription around the bowl reading 'Menhir me fecit in Tempore Genillan' (Made in the time of Gennillan, lord of Ystrad Yw in the mid-eleventh century).

Square fonts cut from a single block of stone, such as the highly decorated twelfth-century font at Lenton (Nottinghamshire), belong in the same overall class with tub fonts. From the round tub developed the round font bowl on a narrower stone pedestal with a separate moulded base. This was often given additional support at the corners by detached shafts, giving a square overall appearance. Cornwall has an impressive series of these fonts, including at Bodmin, St Austell and Roche. Square

88 Shernborne (Norfolk) has a sophisticated Norman font in a church that is otherwise not recognisable as ancient. It has attached columns at the angles of the bowl with twisted decoration similar to that introduced at Durham Cathedral in the late eleventh century. Around the underside of the bowl are masks emitting stylised foliage, an early example of the 'green men' found later in the Middle Ages

fonts were also sometimes given corner shafts, like the well-known Norfolk examples at Burnham Deepdale and Shernborne (*88, 91*).

Most fonts were carved from freestone. A small number of fonts are constructed of cast lead. A cluster of them in Gloucestershire, such as at Frampton-on-Severn and Slimbridge, suggests that there was a foundry in Bristol producing them. They are also found in other parts of southern England and as far north as Ashover (Derbyshire). A select group of churches have fonts sculpted from polished black marble from Tournai on the Franco-Belgian border. These fonts, including at East Meon (Hampshire), and at Winchester and Lincoln cathedrals, were imported from France and their similarity of design suggest they were the product of a single workshop. At least one church, Marks Tey (Essex), has a wooden font.

'Hoc fontis sacro pereunt delicta lavacro' is the inscription around the rim of the font at Lullington (Somerset) – in this holy font the sins of the world are washed away. These sins were represented symbolically as mythical beasts and serpents, which have often been misinterpreted as pagan symbols. The tub font at Avebury (Wiltshire) shows both a dragon and a bishop holding a crozier; Bodmin (Cornwall) has mythical beasts in combat, a favourite theme of Norman carvers; Shernborne (Norfolk)

Left: 89 Toller Fratrum
(Dorset) font is a tub-
shaped basin with a group
of enigmatic relief figures
with arms aloft

Opposite: 90 The Norman
font at West Haddon
(Northamptonshire) has
Biblical scenes including
Christ's entry into
Jerusalem

has an early form of green man lurking on the underside of the bowl
(*88*). Much of the carving is of primitive figures, for example at Luppitt
(Devon) where there are stylised human and beast heads, or the group of
figures at Toller Fratrum (Dorset) who might represent a community of
Christian souls, or might be sinners waving in distress (*89*).

   The work of the Herefordshire school of carvers, already described in
the architecture of Kilpeck, also includes some exceptional fonts. In the
quality of their carving and their subject matter these fonts show a much
greater level of sophistication than the majority of contemporary works,
reflecting the sophisticated tastes of their patrons. Eardisley (Herefordshire)
font, contemporary with the church that was probably built in the period
1135–42, shows two knights in combat amid the evil forces of entwin-
ing stems (*colour plate 21*). It has been suggested that they represent a

duel fought in 1127 at which the patron of the church, Sir Ralph de Baskerville, killed his father-in-law. The remainder of the font shows the expiation of sin: it shows Christ's Harrowing of Hell (after his crucifixion Christ descended into hell where he defeated the powers of evil), and a lion. According to the *Bestiaries* the lion had virtuous qualities (and was the emblem of Mark the evangelist). Similar lions also occur on the font at Shobdon (Herefordshire), retained when the church was demolished in 1752 and placed inside the new church. According to the *Bestiaries*, all lion cubs were stillborn and were watched over by their mother for three days, until their father came and breathed life into them.

Castle Frome (Herefordshire) font is similar in style to Eardisley, but the subject matter is different. The font stands on a broad base with three crouching figures beneath or crushed by it. Only one of the faces is intact. The principal theme of the font is the Baptism of Christ, complete with the hand of God and the dove of the Holy Spirit. It also has an angel, lion, bull and eagle, emblems of the four Evangelists. Other exceptional fonts by the same school of carvers are at Stottesdon (Shropshire), Chaddesley Corbet (Worcestershire), which has a frieze of serpentine wyverns, and at Orleton (Herefordshire), which has apostles framed by arches.

Lenton (Nottinghamshire) font was made for a Cluniac Priory on the site and is a square block, the faces of which are carved with Crucifixion, Resurrection and Ascension. Bridekirk (Cumbria) is also a square tub font, depicting the Baptism of Christ but with more primitive tooling than the Herefordshire school. Secular schemes are also sometimes found on fonts, such as the Labours of the Months at Burnham Deepdale (Norfolk) and on the lead font at Brooklands (Kent) (*91*).

Fonts of the thirteenth and fourteenth century are usually less spectacular. Fonts of a similar character at Southrop (Gloucestershire) and Stanton Fitzwarren (Wiltshire) recall the lavishness of Norman fonts (*92*). Both have figures beneath the cusped arches of an arcade. They depict the Psychomachia, in which Virtues, represented by armed virgins, each do battle and triumph over a specific vice. At Stanton Fitzwarren, the names of the vices are carved in Latin on the arches. In other examples Early-English fonts follow the discipline of contemporary architecture. Eaton Bray (Bedfordshire) has a bowl with four detached shafts at the angles, each decorated with a stiff-leaf capital (*93*).

Acton Burnell (Shropshire) has a more sober but elegant arcade of arches. In the fourteenth century there was more variation. Meare and Weston Zoyland (both Somerset) have shaped fonts in which the bowl, stem and base are conceived as a single piece and are ornamented solely with thick

Opposite: 91 Burnham Deepdale (Norfolk) font has a square bowl on a pedestal. It shows the Labours of the Months, an unusual subject for a font

Right: 92 Stanton Fitzwarren (Wiltshire) font is tub-shaped and depicts the Psychomachia, or the struggle between good and evil

93 Eaton Bray (Bedfordshire) has a font contemporary with the thirteenth-century church, in which the square bowl has stiff-leaf capitals on the angle shafts; Gothic treatment of a Norman form

94 Barnack
(Huntingdonshire) has
a fourteenth-century
font with Decorated
embellishment

horizontal bands. Barnack (Huntingdonshire) has low-relief foliage to its
round bowl, standing on a low arcade of cusped arches (*94*). Others have
blind tracery around the bowl, such as at Brailes (Warwickshire).

Octagonal fonts first appear in the fourteenth century, but subsequently they became the most common form. Perpendicular fonts are
legion and follow a standard structure of a panelled steam and an octagonal bowl, the faces of which have low-relief carving. Some are raised
on stepped plinths. The most notable late medieval fonts are the Seven
Sacraments fonts found in East Anglia. The eighth panel was carved with
the crucifixion or some other scene. Binham Priory, Cley, Gresham,
Salle, Walsingham (all Norfolk), Walsoken (Cambridgeshire), Badingham,
Laxfield and Weston (Suffolk) all have fine examples (*95*). Only two such
fonts are found outside of East Anglia, at Nettlecombe (Somerset) and
Farningham (Kent).

95 The octagonal font is typical of the Perpendicular, as in this example from Binham Priory (Norfolk) which is carved with the Seven Sacraments

Although fonts had been covered since the thirteenth century, it was the fifteenth and sixteenth centuries when the font cover or canopy became a feature in its own right. Tall canopies, like open spires, were ornamented with tracery and bedecked with pinnacles. The best examples, like fonts of the period, are in East Anglia – at Sudbury, Ufford (both Suffolk) and Trunch (Norfolk). The canopies are so tall that pulleys are used to lift them to allow them to be used. The practice continued after the Reformation. Terrington St Clement (Norfolk) has an early seventeenth-century cover over its late medieval font.

As baptism maintained its significance after the Reformation, fonts of this period were carefully designed structures. Ornamentation was now in the classical style. Grinling Gibbons (1648-1721) designed several fonts for Wren's London churches, some of which have ornate font covers. Other London churches have elegant small bowls on fluted pedestals. Architects

96 St Swithin, Worcester, was built 1733-35 by Thomas and Edward Woodward. The font is contemporary, a shaped marble pedestal and bowl, too small for immersion, and a mahogany cover

also became font designers. Great Witley (Worcestershire) font has three classically robed women forming its stem, and an elaborate font cover, all possibly the work of James Gibbs. Robert Adam's font at Croome D'Abitot (Worcestershire) and the font at Worcester St Swithin are slender pieces with bowls that are obviously too small for immersion (*96*). Marble and, occasionally also Wedgwood pottery, were used for fonts of this period. Blaenavon (Monmouthshire) was an iron town and its church built in 1805, patronised by the local ironmaster, has an elegant cast-iron font.

Gothic Revival architects also designed fonts and font covers. William Butterfield designed the font at Ottery St Mary (Devon) in 1850 using a mosaic of different coloured marbles to create a strong, patterned effect. Mosaic and materials of different colours – polished marble was especially favoured – characterise the most Victorian of fonts, although Perpendicular style fonts were still reproduced in this period in large numbers. The majority of font covers also belong to the nineteenth

97 The pulpit at Fotheringay
(Northamptonshire) is said to
have been a gift of Edward
IV and is one of the earliest
pulpits to have a surviving
sounding board, or 'tester'

century. Brant Broughton (Lincolnshire) has a tall medieval-style font canopy made in 1889, possibly designed by G.F. Bodley who had already restored the church. The base of the canopy has doors that open to reveal painted panels and carved figures of Saints Michael, Nicholas and Agnes.

PULPITS AND LECTERNS

The Latin *pulpitum* refers to a stage or platform from which the Creed was recited and from which sermons were preached. In parish churches the earliest pulpits belong to the fifteenth century, some time after preaching had become an established, if irregular, feature of worship. The majority are constructed of wood. The 'wineglass' profile of a polygonal pulpit on a thin pedestal was common. The pulpit at Fotheringay (Northamptonshire) is a good example of the style, with a rib-vaulted sounding board, or tester (97).

Left: 98 Trull (Somerset) has a wooden pulpit on a stone base, probably of the early sixteenth century. It has figures of St John and the Four Doctors of the Church (Saints Gregory, Augustine of Hippo, Jerome and Ambrose)

Opposite: 99 Monksilver (Somerset) retains one of the very few medieval wooden eagle lecterns

The pulpit has been repainted, but others retain traces of their original paint. At Horsham St Faith (Norfolk) original painted saints have survived, a form of decoration very close to the dado of a rood screen. Others had sculpted wooden figures in niches. The pulpit at Long Sutton (Somerset) has replacement figures of the Apostles. Trull (Somerset) has large figures of the Four Doctors of the western church, and of St John the Evangelist (*98*). It is a polygonal structure but was designed to stand on a stone base. This form of design is also found in Devon.

There are several surviving masonry pulpits from before the Reformation. A group found in the Mendip Hills of Somerset, such as Shepton Mallet and Banwell, are from the same school of carvers. There are also several examples in Devon and in Gloucestershire, such as Cirencester, Northleach and Chedworth.

Lecterns were used to support the liturgical books during the Mass. The most common medieval form was a wooden or brass eagle on a pedestal, very few of which have survived. Monksilver (Somerset)

and Astbury (Cheshire) retain wooden lecterns; Yeovil (Somerset) and Chipping Camden (Gloucestershire) have brass eagle lecterns of the early sixteenth century (*99*). After the Reformation lecterns were moved to the nave and used for reading the Epistle and Gospels. That eagle lecterns are familiar is entirely due to the nineteenth century when countless medieval-style lecterns were supplied to parish churches. In the seventeenth and eighteenth centuries, however, the pulpit and lectern (or reading desk) were often either combined or designed to form a pair.

The majority of churches were not furnished with a pulpit until the seventeenth century, which is why Jacobean-style pulpits are the most common form of pre-Victorian pulpit (*100*). Usually but not necessarily hexagonal, they feature round arches and low-relief ornamentation known as strapwork. Most had a tester, although these rarely survive. Combining the pulpit and reading desk resulted in what are known as double-decker pulpits. Three-decker pulpits, much more rare, had a desk for the parish clerk forming the lower tier. The pulpit was usually positioned at the east end of the nave, but there was a fashion in the eighteenth century for moving the pulpit half way along the north or south wall, in a manner adopted by nonconformist chapels. At Teigh (Rutland) the pulpit is set against the west wall.

100 The Jacobean pulpit and tester at Tintinull (Somerset) is typical of seventeenth-century work, with its round arches and profuse low-relief decoration

Come the Anglican Revival, architects regularly designed pulpits as part of an integral approach to the interior furnishings. Victorian architects designed pulpits based on their medieval predecessors, but they also introduced a level of opulence in pulpit design not seen in the Middle Ages, where use of polychrome masonry offered effects unavailable to medieval masons. However, many Victorian pulpits are the product of individual donations and are designed to suit the tastes of their donors.

BENCHES AND PEWS

Originally there were no seats in the nave. Worshippers were required to stand or kneel during the entire performance of the Mass. Nave and aisles were used for processions and secular functions that would have inhibited the way that any seating was arranged. By tradition ledges were built along the walls and at the base of arcade piers which allowed the old or infirm to rest while attending the Mass. Benches became common in the later Middle Ages for a variety of reasons. They represent a desire for greater comfort in the church and reflect the growing importance of sermons. Their installation was made possible by removal of many secular functions to the churchyard or to separate church houses.

Dunsfold (Surrey) has thirteenth-century benches that are the oldest known benches in a British church. Most pre-Reformation benches, however, belong to the fifteenth and sixteenth centuries. They are particularly rewarding to study because of the wealth of carvings found on the bench ends. Since most of the subject matter of these carvings was secular, and the religious themes included few saints that were vulnerable to destruction at the Reformation, bench ends form one of the best-preserved groups of medieval wood carving.

Two makers of benches recorded their names on their work, a rare practice among medieval craftsman. Altarnun (Cornwall) has a bench

101 Broomfield (Somerset) has benches of the mid-sixteenth century carved by Simon Werman, whose preference for foliage and vines is well represented here

with the inscription 'Robart Daye Maker of this work', but unfortunately the date is no longer legible. Broomfield and Trull (Somerset) have mid-sixteenth-century bench ends signed by Simon Werman (*101*). Werman lived at Bicknoller on the Quantock Hills. His work can be identified by the particular form of edge moulding that he favoured and his career encompassed pre- and post-Reformation churches.

Although benches sometimes have carved backs and fronts, it is the bench end that was the focus of attention. Bench ends follow two basic designs. They are either square-headed, or the top is curved up and crowned by a finial known as a poppy head. The former type is most common in south-west England, the latter in East Anglia. In most cases decoration was applied in relief to a large panel. But the armrests could also be used for sculpted figures or animals. At Wiggenhall St Mary and Wiggenhall St Germans (Norfolk) can be found the most sumptuously carved benches in Britain (*102*). They feature saints in high relief on pedestals, which are in niches below the poppy head, while the armrests have figures representing the virtues and vices.

102 The bench ends at Wiggenhall St Mary (Norfolk), with saints in niches and figures on the arm rests, are the most sumptuously carved examples of their type

Some religious subjects were copied from printed books. The Resurrection at Hatch Beauchamp (Somerset), another work by Simon Werman, was copied from the *Biblia Pauperum*, or 'poor man's Bible'. The unusual portrayal of Joshua and Caleb at Milverton (Somerset) has the same source (*103*). Symbols of Christ's Passion – including hammer and nails, spear, sponge, ladder and the five wounds of Christ – are also a common religious theme, with many examples in Cornwall. Virtue and vice was another popular subject, the best-known sets being at Wiggenhall St Germans mentioned above, and Blythburgh (Suffolk). The devil also appears, at Freckenham (Suffolk) consigning the damned to the jaws of hell (*104*). In addition, many of the animals and beasts depicted on bench ends were derived from the *Bestiaries*, in which all animals have moral attributes. Dragons and wyverns represented the Devil (*colour plate 22*). Mermaids were temptresses ready to steal way the souls of virtuous men. A more curious creature, found only at Dennington (Suffolk), is a sciapod, a mythical desert creature who used his large foot as a parasol. The pelican was a symbol of Christ because, again according to the

103 At Milverton (Somerset) a bench shows the figures of Joshua and Caleb returning from the Promised Land, a scene taken from the Book of Numbers

104 At Freckenham (Suffolk) the devil
shoves the damned into the jaws of Hell

Bestiaries, she strikes and kills her disrespectful offspring. After three days she pierces her breast and restores them to life with her own blood. The image was therefore a metaphor for Christ's sacrifice for humankind.

Secular subjects give a glimpse of contemporary medieval life. At Ixworth Thorpe (Suffolk) is a thatcher with his rake and knife. Somerset bench ends have many secular subjects, including the windmill and miller at Bishops Lydeard, boys climbing trees at East Lyng and a fuller at Spaxton, part of a set dated 1536. Bagpipers, fiddlers, jesters and contortionists are all found on Cornish bench ends, like those of Davidstow and St Levan. These are not easy to date precisely and some of them may belong to the later sixteenth century after the Reformation. Churches were furnished with benches throughout the sixteenth century and they remained essentially medieval in character. Devon churches such as Monkleigh and Down St Mary have heraldic designs or initials, probably of the donors, while at North Cadbury (Somerset) traditional religious themes like Passion symbols are in the same set of benches with Renaissance-style heads in profile.

Early seventeenth-century benches are structurally similar to medieval benches, but in the Jacobean style (strictly speaking belonging to the reign of James I, 1603-25). This northern Renaissance style familiar from pulpits and screens (and domestic woodwork) has round-headed panels, sometimes crowned by shells instead of finials. Good examples are at Walpole St Peter (Norfolk). Benches would later become an integral part of the interior design of the church. Shobdon (Herefordshire) has bench ends purposefully designed as part of a complete interior Rococo Gothic scheme of the eighteenth century (*colour plate 10*).

Church seating in the seventeenth and eighteenth centuries expressed and reinforced the social hierarchy. It was in this period that pew renting became popular. Families were able to rent their own pews, providing extra income for the parish, while the poor had to make do with humbler benches at the rear, or escape to the local dissenting chapel. The most ostentatious of the private family pews had curtains and upholstered chairs. The private pew to some extent fulfilled one of the functions of the former chantry chapels, in expressing social superiority. In a post-Reformation church it served to focus attention on both the priest and the squire. At Moreton Corbet (Shropshire) the church stands adjacent to a now ruinous Elizabethan mansion, and in the church the Corbet family pew is railed off from the south aisle, and contains the family memorials. Stokesay (Shropshire) also stands close to a large fortified medieval house. In the church the squire's pew is a mid-seventeenth-century canopied pew, still Jacobean in style, at the east end of the nave closest to the pulpit. Galleries also housed private pews, as at Whitby mentioned below. Rycote (Oxfordshire) was built next to a manor house, which has long since been demolished, but the church retains two canopied pews. Both are enclosed on three sides with arcading above the panels, and with canopies, one housing a musicians' gallery, the other almost an onion dome. The Duke of Chandos had in 1715 a triple-decker gallery pew erected for himself and his servants at Little Stanmore (Greater London).

Box pews grew out of a desire for more comfort in the church, in a period when the sermon took precedence over the Eucharist and required the congregation to sit for long periods. At first doors were added between existing bench ends. In London, churches built after the Great Fire had pews of this type. The box pew is itself higher, dividing the nave into a series of compartments. Some of them had, and still have, names or numbers painted on them, a reference to their owners. They were arranged so as to focus on the pulpit rather than the altar, which often meant a wholesale clearance when the interior was re-ordered in the nineteenth century and when pew renting was abolished.

105 Diserth (Powys) has box pews either side of the sanctuary (one dated 1687) that were intended partly to de-mystify the east end of the church. The restored altar rails are also of the late seventeenth century

Pre-Victorian interiors have been much prized by church historians, Whitby (North Yorkshire) being one of the most celebrated. Two of the best examples where the seating is arranged to face the pulpit are at Compton Wynyates (Warwickshire) and Diserth (Powys) (*105*).

Victorian benches reproduced the late medieval style where there were funds available. Elsewhere architects introduced much plainer soft-wood benches mass-produced to standard designs, many of which are themselves now deemed outmoded. Clearance of earlier seating was done on the grounds of changing fashion, but also when the earlier seating had rotted. Modern churches are likely to have moveable chairs so as to allow greater flexibility over the use of the interior.

CHOIR STALLS AND MISERICORDS

In a medieval church, choir stalls were set up in the chancel for monks and secular canons. The rule of St Benedict required these priests to sing the daily offices of the church – matins, lauds, prime, terce, sext, nones, vespers and compline – standing up. To ease the burden of standing for long periods wooden ledges on the underside of hinged seats, known as misericords, allowed the priests to lean back and take the weight off their feet, while remaining in an upright position.

Choir stalls and misericords exist in parish churches only under certain circumstances. In some cases a parish church was shared with a monastery, like Christchurch Priory (Dorset), where the misericords have survived. Other monastic churches achieved parochial status at the Reformation. Collegiate churches also had misericords and were more often shared with parishes. The majority of misericords in parish churches are therefore a leftover from the building's former collegiate status. In other cases, stalls and misericords from redundant monasteries were salvaged for use by a local parish church, probably mainly for the practical reason that they were well-made seats in good condition. Beaumaris (Anglesey) and Whalley (Lancashire) are good examples where complete sets survive.

106 Ludlow St Laurence (Shropshire) was a large town church with many guild chaplains who formed a college. Their misericords, all of *c.*1447, include one depicting an owl, symbolising ignorance because it preferred darkness to the light of Christianity

Choir stalls were arranged in tiers of seats facing each other on the north and south sides of the chancel, and often extending in an L-shape across the west side of the chancel as well. Design of the stall ends was similar to the design of bench ends already described. The seats themselves had curved backs with arms rests and, occasionally, were under elaborate wooden canopies, of which Whalley, mentioned above, is a good example (although the ensemble of stalls, misericords and canopy is best seen in cathedral churches).

The seat is a single piece of wood, the underside of which is a ledge on a corbel-like projection. The projection is carved, and has subsidiary carvings, known as supporters, to the right and left. The most common subject matter of misericords is foliage. Religious subjects are uncommon, and were hardly appropriate for priests to sit on. Allegorical and secular scenes are more plentiful and constitute one of the major sources of surviving medieval wood carving. Allegorical scenes were drawn from the *Bestiaries*, like the unicorn on a misericord at Greystoke (Cumbria), and the owl at Ludlow (Shropshire) (*106*).

Cartmel Priory (Cumbria) has an entertaining set of real and imaginary animals including pelican, elephant and castle, unicorn, hart, a monkey holding a urinal (a satirical jibe at the medical profession) and a mermaid. It also has a tricephalos, a three-headed king representing the Devil, with foliage spewing from his right and left mouths (*107*). More conventional green men are also sometimes found on misericords, such as the supporters on misericords at Ludlow and Tong (Shropshire), but the best example is the mid-fourteenth-century green man at King's Lynn St Margaret (Norfolk). Ludlow also has some fine secular scenes, probably drawn from the Labours of the Months, a sequence that survives complete at Ripple (Worcestershire) (*108*). These scenes were probably copied from books such as calendars and psalters. Domestic strife was another favourite theme and is the subject of misericords at Fairford (Gloucestershire) and Lavenham (Suffolk).

Misericords were not a special target of Reformation iconoclasts. Nevertheless, comparatively few have survived the re-ordering of chancels over successive centuries. Discarding of misericords even continued during the Anglican revival of the nineteenth century when misericords were removed from King's Lynn St Nicholas (Norfolk) that fortuitously

107 Misericords at Cartmel Priory (Cumbria) include a tricephalos, a three-headed figure of the Devil. The outer faces are green men spewing vegetation

108 Misericords at Ripple (Worcestershire) form a complete set of the Labours of the Months. This scene depicts reaping in August

found their way to the Victoria and Albert Museum. The organisation of the chancel with stalls at its west end was reintroduced by Victorian architects, largely made possible by the development of church music and the desirability of a choir to lead the singing. Victorian choir stalls are similar to their medieval counterparts although, like pews in the nave, financial constraints caused many to be purchased to standard designs.

ORGANS

There has always been music in churches. In the medieval church the Mass was sung by the priests, in part because a singing voice had greater projection than a spoken voice, and plainsong thus became a useful attribute in a large building. Trained choirs were a feature only of higher-status churches. Plainsong was familiar in parish churches, for which organs were sometimes installed and used by priests. Most of these organs were portable and could therefore be used to provide musical accompaniment for processions. Organ-playing was declared one of the 'faults and abuses of religion' in 1536 and declined after the Reformation, with a brief revival under Archbishop Laud in the 1630s. Puritans maintained that instrumental music was a distraction to divine worship and in 1644 passed an Act of Parliament requiring the removal of organs from all parish churches.

Very few organs have survived from the period before the Restoration. A sixteenth-century organ, its case decorated with linenfold panelling, has survived at Old Radnor (Powys) (*109*). Stanford-on-Avon (Northamptonshire) has a seventeenth-century organ installed high against the nave wall (*colour plate 23*). Others are at Winchcombe (Gloucestershire) and Framlingham (Suffolk), the latter acquired from Pembroke College, Cambridge.

Church organs began to appear in parish churches after the Restoration, especially in affluent and urban churches. Rebuilding of London churches after the Great Fire saw the installation of new organs, chiefly by immigrant organ builders such as Bernhard Schmidt and Renatus Harris. Original organs have survived at St Stephen Walbrook, St Clement Eastcheap, St Magnus London Bridge and St Sepulchre Holborn. St Mary Redcliffe, Bristol, boasted in the late eighteenth century the only parochial church organ with pedals. George I donated £1500 to an organ at St Martin-in-the-Fields, London in

109 The Elizabethan organ case at Old Radnor (Powys) displays the contemporary fashion for linenfold panelling

1726 (now at Wotton-under-Edge in Gloucestershire). At Great Witley (Worcestershire), a Georgian estate church with interior scheme of 1747, the organ is an integral component of the west side of the nave. Its case was acquired from the sale of chapel furniture from Cannons near London. The impulse behind these developments was high-church tastes and the more genteel desire for more accomplished musicianship to dignify the service. Congregational hymn singing was pioneered by nonconformists and Methodists, who formed a tendency within the Church of England before formally separating in 1791.

Nevertheless, organs in parish churches mostly date from the late nineteenth century. It has been estimated that in 1800 less than 10 per cent of parish churches had an organ. Organs were expensive and required a trained musician to play them. The alternative was to employ a band of players, featuring usually strings and woodwind. They performed in west galleries or sometimes in the rood loft. In Thomas Hardy's *Under the Greenwood Tree* (1872) replacement of the traditional players by a church organ played by a formally trained musician is the principal sub-plot of the novel. It was a significant social as well as religious change. Not all of the organs installed in the late nineteenth century were fixed – smaller harmoniums were also employed. Organs were installed concurrent with choir stalls, and often had cases designed by the architect to integrate with the whole chancel scheme. Studley Royal (North Yorkshire) has an organ supplied by T.C. Lewis of London, the two-tier case of which, complete with arcading and a jettied upper tier, was designed by William Burges and is a magnificent imposing piece that dominates the nave.

CIVIC PARAPHERNALIA

Stands for ceremonial paraphernalia, such as maces, mayoral insignia and swords, were introduced into parish churches from the late seventeenth century. The stands were constructed of wrought iron, influenced by secular Baroque ironwork. Numerous Bristol, London and Norwich churches have good examples. A stand for mayoral insignia at Wilton (Wiltshire) is dated 1677. Warwick St Mary has a mace rest by Nicholas Parris, contemporary with the substantial rebuilding of the church at the end of the seventeenth century.

POOR BOXES AND DOLE CUPBOARDS

Dole cupboards are sometimes found on the wall of the nave or aisles. They were designed to hold bread for distribution to the poor. Nearly all of them are post-Reformation, examples of which can be seen at Warwick St Mary and at Ruislip (Greater London). Poor boxes are another feature usually dated after the Reformation. These simple boxes, many of which bear the legend 'Remember the Poor', date mainly from the seventeenth and eighteenth centuries. Blythburgh (Suffolk) has a late medieval poor box with traceried panels.

8

DEATH AND MEMORY

SHRINES

Relics were the bones of saints or objects associated with their lives. In popular religion they retained the living essence of the saint who, being closer to God, gave special sanctity to the buildings in which they were housed. When Pope Gregory I sent Abbot Mellitus on his missionary journey to England in 601 he instructed him to ensure that relics were deposited in every parish church that he founded. Altars and relics were deemed essential to the sanctity of the building even at this early date. In practice relics subsequently came to enjoy a cult status and attracted pilgrims on various kinds of journey. Prayers of supplication were offered at their shrines in the hope of a cure for all manner of ailments, absolution of sins (pilgrimage was a common form of penance), or even spiritual guidance, accompanied by an offering. It made relics a profitable form of business. Benedictine monasteries in particular cultivated the cult of relics, most notably when Glastonbury Abbey was being built at the end of the twelfth century and the bones of Arthur were conveniently discovered. Some relics were of Biblical saints and were brought back to Britain following pilgrimages or Crusades in the Holy Land. Others were the bones of native saints who had been canonised by the popes. It is self-evident that few of these relics could have been genuine.

Relics were dignified by housing them in highly ornate boxes of wood or metal, known as reliquaries (see 3). In this form they were paraded in processions at religious festivals, especially at the saint's patronal festival. To receive pilgrims it was more practical to house the reliquary in a permanent shrine. These were usually in the form of tombs, the appearance of which was based the tombs of the early martyrs.

155

Relics were venerated, although the Protestants maintained they were worshipped, for which reason they were suppressed at the Reformation. Most surviving shrines are in churches of high status – Edward the Confessor at Westminster Abbey, Thomas Beckett at Canterbury Cathedral, St David at St Davids Cathedral. The oldest shrine in Britain, however, is at the remote church of Pennant Melangell (Powys), which houses the relics of Melangell. Melangell (*Monacella* in Latin) is said to have been abbess of a monastery near Llangynog (Powys) in the seventh century. The wooden shrine housing her relics dates to the twelfth century, although it has been reconstructed from pieces retained after it was originally broken up. At Whitchurch Canonicorum (Dorset) the shrine housing the remains of St Wite is a plain stone tomb chest with three mandorla-shaped openings, probably for offerings. A stone chest at St Endellion (Cornwall) is of Catacleuse stone and is finely carved with vaulted niches under ogee arches. Now used as the altar, it was probably originally a shrine to St Endelienta (*110*).

110 The present altar at St Endellion (Cornwall) was probably originally the base of a shrine to St Endelienta

TOMBS AND MONUMENTS

Nearly every church has a funerary monument of some kind, while some churches are simply choc-a-bloc with them. Monuments are a rewarding subject for numerous reasons: they tell us about changing attitudes to death over many centuries; they reveal the self-image of the people they commemorate; they are related to contemporary architecture, often less defined by regional styles than the buildings they are housed in; they constitute the majority of surviving figure sculpture from the medieval and post-Reformation period; and they tell us about contemporary dress and the changing forms of other visual symbolism, including heraldry.

Permanent memorials inside churches began as a decorated grave slabs, usually with no more decoration than a foliated cross. Northampton St Peter has a richly carved coffin lid of the late twelfth century with stylised foliage, monsters and a green man, but it is exceptional. From the end of the twelfth-century effigies carved in high relief on coffin slabs first appear in churches and monasteries. Monuments composed of full-scale sculpted likenesses on tomb chests became a fixture of parish churches by the end of the thirteenth century and remained so in various forms until the nineteenth century. In the twentieth century monuments declined as a form of commemoration. Instead, memorials took the form of stained glass windows, church furniture or screens.

EFFIGIES

Fully articulated recumbent effigies appear in parish churches from the mid-thirteenth century and remained popular well into the seventeenth century. Effigies show the individual in the prime of life and, in order for the sculptors to depict their subjects in the finest possible detail, high-quality stone was essential. Derbyshire alabaster was the stone most sought after for fine carving, although other local stones, especially the fine-grained limestones, were also suitable. Wood was rarely used. Originally the effigies were painted and gilded for heightened effect. Gilt bronze was even rarer as it was a luxury item, and the best example in a parish church is the effigy of Richard Beauchamp, earl of Warwick (died 1439), which stands in the centre of the chantry chapel at Warwick St Mary.

Effigies of knights are the most common form of early funeral monument, and the elite continued to portray themselves as warriors until the sixteenth century (*111*). One of the earliest effigies in a parish church, at Stowe-Nine-Churches (Northamptonshire), shows the emerging fashion for depicting knights with crossed legs. There is no substance to the myth that effigies with crossed legs refer to crusaders. Knights reach for their swords or, with their wives, are shown at prayer. Their heads rest on helmets or cushions, often with some relevant heraldic device. Their feet rest on lions or other heraldic beasts. Thirteenth-century effigies show the knight in a full suit of chain mail, but only rarely with the great helm worn over the head, which obscured the face. In the fourteenth century plate armour was introduced, along with spurs and the bascinet – a pointed helmet with mail hanging down around the neck. Armour became more simplified in the sixteenth century, at a time when its importance diminished with the emergence of firearms.

Effigies of men in civilian dress are uncommon before the fourteenth century. Much Marcle (Herefordshire) has a male effigy in wood of

111 The late fourteenth-century knight effigy of Sir Humphrey Littlebury at Holbeach (Lincolnshire) has been attributed to a Bristol craftsman. His head rests on a helmet. The tomb chest has deep arched niches, originally with figures

112 The effigies of Chief Justice Bromley (died 1555) and Lady Bromley at Wroxeter (Shropshire). He is shown in his robes of office

*c.*1360. Effigies depict the important professions, such as judges, including the fifteenth-century alabaster figure of Sir William Gascoine at Harewood (North Yorkshire), and Lord Chief Justice Bromley (died 1555) at Wroxeter (Shropshire) (*112*). At Skegsby (Nottinghamshire) is a fourteenth-century effigy of a forest official. Priests are less commonly commemorated in parish than in monastic or cathedral churches. They are usually depicted wearing their Mass vestments.

Women were less commonly represented, although the effigy of a woman at Wolferlow (Herefordshire) belongs to the mid-thirteenth century and is one of the earliest of such monuments. Women are often commemorated side by side with their husbands. Their hands are at prayer, and their feet rest upon lap dogs or puppies. Women are also sometimes shown holding hearts, as at Gonalston (Nottinghamshire), and are often dressed in 'widows weeds'. Otherwise female effigies wear the gowns and head dresses fashionable in their day. One of the finest female effigies is of Lady Brereton (died 1522) at Malpas (Cheshire), who wears a high head dress with pointed peaks, and has hair flowing down over the shoulders.

TOMB CHESTS, RAILINGS AND CANOPIES

Monuments gained a specific architectural context, and a sense of permanence, when they were placed in specially constructed arched recesses. Recesses would eventually be superseded by the chantry chapel as the essential context for a monument. It seems likely that the rear of the recesses was painted with religious or other scenes, although only a handful of fragmentary remains have now survived. At Maidstone (Kent) the monument to John Wotton (died 1417) has a painted representation of the deceased being presented to the Virgin Mary. Monuments also achieved more presence by mounting them on tomb chests, which were either designed to be placed in a recess, or were intended to be free-standing and visible from all four sides. In practice most medieval tomb chests have been moved around on several occasions.

Tomb chests, derived from the design of shrines, were ideal for decoration, which usually comprised blind arcading or rows of niches (*111*). These framed the shields of arms, miniature standing figures of people

113 The alabaster tomb of Sir Richard Vernon (died 1451) and his wife, on a tomb chest with carved angels and saints, at Tong (Shropshire)

associated with the deceased known as 'weepers', and angels or saints (*113*). Weepers were either standing figures (sometimes holding shields as at Ewelme (Oxfordshire)), or kneeling in prayer. Towards the end of the medieval period a fashion emerged for open tomb chests. The effigy would be placed on the slab in the conventional manner, but beneath it was a 'cadaver', a representation of the deceased as a decaying corpse wrapped in a burial shroud. Notable examples are the tombs of John Earl of Arundel (died 1435) at Arundel (Sussex) and Sir John Golafre (died 1442) at Fyfield (Berkshire). Cadavers were a public show of humility and reminded onlookers of the fate awaiting everyone. This gruesome depiction of death would persist in Renaissance and post-Reformation monuments.

Later medieval monuments adopted architectural pretensions in the form of canopies, some freestanding, others an extension of the arched recess. Good early examples of the wall canopy, where the arch is enclosed within a gable, can be seen in the early fourteenth-century monuments at Winchelsea (East Sussex), including the tomb of Stephen Alard (died *c.*1300), admiral of the cinque ports. An alternative design was to set the arch between two pinnacled shafts, as at the de la Beche monuments at Aldworth (Berkshire) of the mid-fourteenth century. Freestanding monuments have vaulted canopies, and date mainly from the fifteenth century onwards. At Melbury Sampford (Dorset) monuments to William Browning (died 1467) and Sir Giles Strangways (died 1547) have Purbeck marble canopies with four-centred arches and panelled undersides. The monument to Sir Henry Vernon (died 1515) at Tong (Shropshire) has an elliptical panelled arch which is effectively an arch between nave and chantry chapel, and has brackets for figures, the heads of which are broken off. At Great Brington (Northamptonshire), the canopy over the tomb of John Spencer (died 1522) stands on freestanding shafts enclosing the tomb chest.

Tombs were given greater dignity and status if they were fenced off by means of iron railings, a symbolic as well as a physical barrier. Iron was an expensive luxury in medieval Britain and conspicuous consumption is part of the message that railings conveyed. Tomb railings of the period are relatively simple. The railings around the tomb at Stanton Harcourt (Oxfordshire) have fleur-de-lis finials, the most popular and aesthetically satisfying way of terminating the finial. At Thame (Oxfordshire) the Willyam monument of 1559 has fleur-de-lis and simpler spike finials (*114*).

114 The Willyam tomb of 1559 at Thame (Oxfordshire) has iron railings and effigies carved by the Southwark school of Dutch craftsmen

BRASSES

Brass effigies appeared in churches from the end of the thirteenth century and remained popular to the sixteenth century. Metal plates (strictly speaking of latten rather than brass) were imported from Flanders, northern France and the Rhineland, for which reason they are found most commonly in the south-east, East Anglia and as far north as Yorkshire. Their distribution is matched in other parts of Britain by the continuing popularity of low-relief stone grave slabs. The rise and popularity of brasses is only partly explained by proximity to North Sea ports and a dearth of suitable local stone for sculpting. Brasses became fashionable in the fifteenth century (*115*). The tomb of Sir William Vernon (died 1467) at Tong, a church with an unparalleled display of freestone and alabaster family monuments, has a tomb chest on which are brass instead of sculpted effigies.

Brasses were usually laid on the ground flush with the surface, but they are also found on tomb chests and set vertically into walls. The deceased are usually represented in the form of a small-scale recumbent effigy

115 The brass to Sir Giles Daubenay (died 1445) and his wife at South Petherton (Somerset) has figures under gables, as if portrayed in a standing position

engraved into the metal, similar in style and dress to sculpted effigies. Early examples include the brass to Sir John d'Abernon (died 1277) at Stoke D'Abernon (Surrey), at Trumpington (Cambridgeshire) and at Acton (Suffolk), although precise dates are not known. Brasses became larger over time and show a stylistic development independent of three-dimensional effigies. Later in the medieval period the relative scale of the figures decreased, figures were set within two-dimensional canopied niches, and thus appeared to be standing rather than lying, or were shown only from the waist upwards, a feature also found on late medieval grave slabs.

RENAISSANCE MONUMENTS

The Renaissance style emerged in Britain in the sixteenth century. Its first flourish was in the form of funeral monuments and it has been argued that monuments constitute the earliest Renaissance architecture in Britain. Renaissance influence in monument design emerged in a long period of overlap with the Gothic style that produced many hybrid monuments. Their form did not change, with effigies on tomb chests remaining the predominant form, of men and their wives in contemporary dress, on chests with simple classical decoration and heraldry (*colour plate 24*). The more ambitious efforts boasted canopies. Gothic pinnacles, shafts and arches were replaced by classical pilasters, balusters and fluted columns framing panels with new forms of decoration such as wreaths, garlands of leaves and fruit, and shell-heads (semi-circular heads with radial fluting resembling a shell). The tomb of the ninth Lord Cobham (died 1561) at Cobham (Kent) displays exuberance and confidence in the new style, with its Ionic pilasters framing the alabaster figures of kneeling mourners. The new motifs were not handled in a way that the classical world would have recognised. Although the Renaissance had begun in Italy, its appearance in Britain was the result of a slow diffusion, with a consequence that the style in Britain was closer to that of northern Europe than to contemporary Italy. This was compounded in the latter half of the sixteenth century when there was an influx of Dutch craftsmen fleeing religious persecution in their homeland. There was an enclave of Dutch monumental masons in Southwark, London, although others settled elsewhere. Therefore many of the features characteristic of the Renaissance style in Britain, such as the low-relief decoration of surfaces, known as strapwork, are Dutch in origin. Dutch workshops attracted English apprentices – notably the prominent monument masons of the seventeenth century, Nicholas Stone and Epiphanius Evesham – with a result that the style gradually disseminated. Some of these Dutch mason-sculptors are known by their Anglicised names – William Cure, Isaac James and Gerard Johnson.

Renaissance decoration was also applied to canopied wall monuments. Towards the end of the sixteenth century freestanding canopied monuments achieved a more architectural treatment. They exhibit the basic forms of classical architecture: columns supporting a horizontal frieze with a more ornate cornice, known as the entablature. Sir William Sharington's (died 1553) monument at Lacock (Wiltshire), which is dated 1566, has a tomb chest without effigies, framed by superstructures outlined by pilasters and entablature, crowned by a shield of arms held aloft by cherubs. Sir Robert Dormer's (died 1552) monument at Wing (Buckinghamshire) features a sarcophagus without effigy, framed by paired columns supporting a deep entablature that projects well in front of the tomb.

Under Dutch influence freestanding monuments incorporated columns supporting round arches with panelled (more correctly known as 'coffered') ceilings or entablatures. At Turvey (Buckinghamshire) the tomb of Lord Mordaunt (died 1571) is surrounded by eight columns on high square bases, forming two bays to each side, supporting an entablature crowned by shields of arms. The whole ensemble resembles a classical temple. The Sydenham monument at Stogumber (Somerset) is a slight variation of this composition: its tomb chest and effigies are beneath a canopy of two arched bays.

THE SEVENTEENTH AND EIGHTEENTH CENTURIES

Freestanding monuments declined in the seventeenth century, superseded by the fashion for wall monuments. Some of these were on a much grander scale than previously, with a result that the social elite dominated the interior appearance of the church in a way that it had not done before (*colour plate 25*). The early seventeenth century saw other gradual shifts in style. White and black marble became the preferred material for monument construction after 1600. There was also an increased repertoire of decorative features. Obelisks, derived ultimately from ancient Egypt, symbolised eternity; cherubs represented spiritual immortality and were sometimes shown blowing trumpets, to raise the dead at the Day of Judgement; women in classical robes symbolised the virtues of the deceased. Urns represented death, but if shown with emerging flames they also represented immortality. Skulls and hourglasses, usually placed lower down the monument, symbolised the transitory nature of earthly existence.

From the seventeenth century most monuments were set against the wall, and included sculpted representations of the deceased against a screen or reredos, with the whole composition crowned by a heraldic achievement – a full achievement would include shield, helmet, crest, mantling and motto. The back plate above the tomb chest was ideal for placing an inscription in English or Latin. Use of English reflected the growing importance of literacy following the Reformation; Latin remained important as a mark of education when the gulf between polite and vernacular culture was growing. Nevertheless the persistence of symbolic decoration and of heraldry demonstrates that Protestant England and Wales remained a strongly visual culture.

Recumbent effigies on tomb chests gradually fell out of favour, although there were developments in the style of later effigies, such as the more realistic portrayal of the deceased, where death is represented as sleep. Nicholas Stone's effigy of Lady Carey (died 1617) at Stowe-Nine-Churches (Northamptonshire) is a tour de force of this style. Contemporary dress in the seventeenth century included the ruff around the neck, worn by both men and women, and the men dressed in ceremonial armour of the type established by Henry VIII. Effigies were also used that adopt a reclining posture. The best example is the remarkable pair of monuments to the Fettiplace family at Swinbrook (Oxfordshire), the earlier of c.1613 and the later erected by William Bird in 1686. Each monument has three tiers of reclining figures, dressed archaically as medieval knights, in a pose that now looks unintentionally comical.

116 The monument to Robert Pierrepont (died 1669) is by John Bushnell and stands in the former chantry of an otherwise demolished church at West Dean (Wiltshire). The deceased is assisted to heaven by an angel, and is within an elaborate Baroque frame with wooden doors

One alternative to the effigy was to portray the deceased as a kneel-ing figure at a prayer desk, a convention of late medieval France that was popularised by Dutch craftsmen. Where husband and wife are both commemorated, they were usually shown kneeling and facing each other with, sometimes, a tier of kneeling children beneath them. There were several alternatives. At Lynsted (Kent) Epiphanius Evesham designed the monument of Lord Teynham (died 1622) with a recumbent effigy of the deceased, behind which and framed by a round arch, is a figure of his mourning wife at prayer. Full-length standing or seated figures in con-temporary dress became current in the seventeenth century; demi-figures and busts also became popular from the second half of the century (116). Another alternative, that found favour into the eighteenth century, was to have a standing wall monument without effigies or busts.

A smaller kind of monument that gained favour from the end of the sixteenth century was the hanging wall monument wholly suspended from the wall. These were smaller than floor-mounted monuments and were used where there was insufficient space (for example when earlier large dominant monuments had taken up most of the available space) or where a grand monument was inappropriate. Stylistically they were miniature forms of contemporary standing monuments, with the same architectural conventions. From this class of memorial came the wall tablet with memorial inscription, which became the most common form of memorial in churches (117). Inscriptions on oval or rectangu-lar tablets were set in architectural frames, or elaborate scrolls known as cartouches. Architectural frames comprised columns, entablature and pediment, with many variations. Tablets were also decorated with the usual array of motifs including garlands, drapes, skulls, cherubs and more, and crowned by a coat of arms or, increasingly in the eighteenth century, by a draped urn.

Renaissance style, based on indirect knowledge of ancient Rome, was replaced by new classical styles based on first-hand knowledge of the ancient world. Of these the Baroque style emerged in the second half of the seventeenth century, contemporary with the architecture of Wren and Hawksmoor. Baroque is a difficult term to pin down, but it can be characterised as a classical form with an exaggerated sense of display and the use of motifs in a manner that was not 'academically' correct. Modifications to the architectural character of monuments included the adoption of the pediment, the transition to white marble

To the Memory of Dr EDWARD CRESSETT
Bishop of *LANDAFF*
second Son of EDWARD CRESSETT *Esqr*
who died Febry 13 1755 in the 58th Year of his Age.
He married first ALBINA the Youngest
Daughter of GRIFFITH RICE of *NEWTON*
in *CARMARTHENSHIRE Esqr* by whom he
had no Issue.
He afterwards married FRANCES the
Eldest Daughter of THOMAS PELHAM *Esqr*
of *LEWES* in *SUSSEX*
by whom he had one Daughter
ELIZABETH who survives him,
to whom he bequeathed his whole Estate

117 A wall tablet by
Thomas Farnolls
Pritchard commemorates
Bishop Edward Cressett
of Llandaf (died 1755) at
Cound (Shropshire). The
mitre and crozier signify
his office

and modification of the decorative vocabulary. Paint was used sparingly
to highlight the design, and for heraldry. Renaissance motifs such as
strapwork, obelisks and the taste for monsters and mermaids declined.
More authentically classical motifs, including cherubs, garlands, urns and
allegorical figures became more prominent, as did the carving in marble
of curtains and drapes.

Monuments also reflect social trends. Opulence and grandeur
expressed the increasing confidence of the aristocracy in the wake of the
restoration of Charles II, and the Baroque style culminated in the ornate
variation of it, known as Rococo, that flourished in the mid-eighteenth
century. This social trend increased with the Whig ascendancy after the
death of Queen Anne in 1714 and the onset of the Hanoverian dynasty.

118 The monument to
Sir William Pole (died
1741) at Shute (Devon)
is a rare eighteenth-
century freestanding
portrait sculpture. It
stands on a pedestal
with commemorative
inscription. The
deceased is portrayed
in contemporary dress
holding a ceremonial
wand of office, referring
to his position as Master
of the Household to
Queen Anne

Britons lived under a king whose powers were limited by Parliament,
giving the aristocracy increasing power. And the height of aristocratic
power in Britain produced its grandest funeral monuments (*118*). One of
the chief characteristics of monuments of the period is the portrayal of
the deceased as Roman citizens, in other words as the heirs of classical
civilisation. Another important factor was the link between the gentry
and the land. With the growing importance of London and the rise of
the town house, it was still imperative for the aristocracy to be commemorated in their ancestral parish church. The earlier monument of
Sir Benjamin Tichborne (died 1621) at Tichborne (Hampshire) has an
inscription recording his service in the court of James I and his desire to
'sleepe with his fathers in this chappell founded by his ancestor'.

The eighteenth century saw increasing diversity in monument design. Purer classical forms – like the Palladianism that had been usurped by Baroque – were a refreshing change from the excesses of Baroque and followed contemporary architectural trends. In fact architects and monument builders were sometimes the same person, as in the case of James Gibbs, who was designing monuments in the second decade of the eighteenth century. Monument design was also influenced by continental trends. Some of the leading monumental sculptors such as Michael Rysbrack (1694-1770), son of an Antwerp painter, the Frenchman Louis Francois Roubiliac (1705-62) and Peter Scheemakers (1691-1781), also from Antwerp, were immigrant craftsmen who gave a fresh impetus to the native scene.

The architectural design of monuments gradually declined. Instead, monumental sculpture was set against a two-dimensional pyramidal background, typically of black marble. It stood on a base with inscription, and formed a controlling shape to the sculpted sarcophagus, on which the deceased and his (rarely her) family were portrayed in antique dress. Rysbrack's monument to the first Lord Foley, completed by 1743, at Great Witley (Worcestershire) is of this classic type. Sarcophagi and urns increased in popularity in the eighteenth century. Although flaming urns had been used since the sixteenth century to symbolise immortality, in the eighteenth century they were fashionably draped to symbolise death, and were often accompanied by a classically robed woman leaning on the urn. These might be mourners, but female figures also symbolised virtue. Weeping willows, with branches drooping over an urn, were an alternative way to express mourning. Symbolism of immortality was a favourite theme of the eighteenth century. At Warkton (Northamptonshire) the duchess of Montagu (died 1775) has discarded her coronet, symbol of earthly status, and is assured of eternal bliss by an angel pointing to heaven. Medallion portraits held aloft by angels or cherubs, such as memorials to Charles Sergison (died 1732) at Cuckfield (Sussex) and John Dalton (died 1791) at Great Stanmore (Greater London), seem to take for granted the promise of eternal life.

THE NINETEENTH CENTURY

The nineteenth century was as varied in its monument design as it was in its architecture. Neo-classical, Greek Revival and Gothic memorials all found favour at different times. The importance of neo-classicism from the latter half of the eighteenth century followed trends in secular architecture led by the likes of Robert Adam. It was also influenced by the discovery by western tourists of Greece and its ancient art and architecture. By asserting the primacy of Greek forms, revivalists were reacting against the decadence of Roman and by extension of showy Baroque and Rococo forms. Although the movement began in Catholic Italy, neo-classicism was in sympathy with the low-church Anglicanism of the period. It introduced sculpture in much lower relief, a lighter touch and a more restrained but elegant approach to decoration. Colour was banished and the purity of white marble held sway.

119 The wall monument to Georgina, Countess of Bradford (died 1842) at Weston-under-Lizard (Staffordshire) was made by John Hollins. The soul of the deceased is carried to heaven by angels. The shallow pediment, which has scrolls at the ends known as acroteria, is typical of the Greek Revival style

Greek revival memorials predominated in the early part of the nineteenth century. Based upon memorial slabs prevalent in Greece, these consisted of a rectangular tablet with inscription and/or relief carving, crowned by a shallow pediment. Grecian style relief carving was given an added impetus by the arrival in London in the early nineteenth century of the Elgin Marbles. On monuments figures are shown in profile in Greek dress. What makes these memorials unmistakably British is the accompanying sentiment. At Badger (Shropshire) the memorial to Harriet Cheney (died 1848) shows the deceased as a seated figure, above which is an angel with outstretched hand ready to lead her up to heaven. In the memorial of Georgina Countess of Bradford (died 1842) by Peter Hollins at Weston-under-Lizard (Staffordshire) the deceased is shown asleep on a couch while angels carry her soul or spirit up to heaven (*119*).

Neo-classical figure sculpture flourished in the early nineteenth century. Less Greek in inspiration, the work of the period has been described as Romantic naturalism. Most of its leading exponents had either worked or travelled in Italy, which became accessible to the British after peace with France in 1815, and which remained pre-eminent in the art world. John Gibson (1790-1866) worked from a studio in Rome; John Flaxman (1755-1826) was professor of sculpture at the Royal Academy, as was Sir Richard Westmacott (1775-1856). Less impressed with Italian art was Sir Francis Chantrey (1781-1841), who specialised in naturalistic portrayals of his subjects somewhere between pathos and sentimentality. His chief works are the reclining figure of Mary Boulton (died 1819) at Great Tew (Oxfordshire), the seated figure of the elderly James Watt (died 1819) at Handsworth (Birmingham) perusing an engine drawing, and the monument of David Pike Watts at Ilam (Staffordshire), completed in 1829, where the semi-reclining figure of the deceased bids farewell to his daughter and her children (*120*). These are all freestanding memorials on plinths.

Gothic monuments predominated after 1850, although Gothic enrichment had been used on many tombs from the late eighteenth century, including the work of Sir Francis Chantrey. Hanging wall monuments were given Gothic architectural frames with cusped arches under high crocketed gables, a type unknown in the medieval period. Recumbent effigies on tomb chests, sometimes beneath canopies, were revived, but in their rich ornamentation were rarely just slavish copies of medieval work, revealing a delight in imaginative ornament. The monument of

120 The monument to David Pike Watts at Ilam (Staffordshire) by Sir Francis
Chantrey was completed in 1829. The deceased is shown in a naturalistic pose
bidding farewell to his daughter and her children

Robert Holford (died 1892) at Westonbirt (Gloucestershire) reveals the love of different materials and their rich effects familiar from fonts and pulpits. Brasses were also revived, to be set into the floor, or a simpler wall-mounted form with inscription.

Victorian monuments are largely devoted to individuals rather than family groups. By the end of the century the grand gesture of the tomb chest had become a rarity. Smaller discreet wall-mounted memorials were more prevalent. But in this period of church building and furnishing, memorials had to compete with bequests that memorialised the individual in other ways – in the form of memorial windows, or the gifts of fonts, pulpits, screens, vestments or plate.

WAR MEMORIALS

War memorials are usually associated with exterior public places, but a number of them are to be found inside churches. They can be personal, regimental or parish memorials. As a maritime and imperial nation, British churches contain numerous memorials to officers who died overseas or at sea. Ships, anchors and nautical instruments accompany seamen; rifles, swords and helmets accompany soldiers. Some of these memorials reveal remarkable personal stories. At Acton Burnell (Shropshire) is the monument to William Smythe (died 1794), killed while fighting with the Austrian cavalry against Republican France. His military background is represented by relief cannon and cannon balls. The Great War brought the need for many more personal memorials, many of which, like Alfred Munnings' equestrian statue commemorating Edward Horner at Mells (Somerset), are important works of art.

Regiments have chapels, often in parish churches, in which memorials record the campaigns in which they fought. St Clement Danes (London) is the chapel of the Royal Air Force. At Shrewsbury St Chad is a memorial chapel of the King's Shropshire Light Infantry and the Herefordshire Regiment. The vestibule of the church has an extensive range of memorials, including a wall monument to those killed during the Indian Mutiny of 1857-9 (*121*).

The most common form of war memorial is the parish memorial. When they are found inside the church they are often no more than a wooden board or brass plaque on which a roll call of the dead has been

121 Shrewsbury St Chad (Shropshire) has numerous regimental war memorials, including this one that commemorates those killed during the Indian Mutiny of 1857-9

painted or engraved. Memorial windows, or a piece of furniture like a chancel screen or reredos, were other popular forms of commemoration. St Mary Swaffham Prior in Cambridge has a memorial window depicting a zeppelin and trench warfare, a rare direct reference. Pontypridd St Catherine (Glamorgan) war memorial west window depicts the patron saints of the four home nations, and represents in Wales the high point of British identity.

HATCHMENTS

Hatchments are diamond-shaped heraldic panels of painted canvas or wood. They were carried in funeral processions to the parish church, and were often displayed at the entrance to the house during a period of mourning. Subsequently they were fixed to the walls of the church, although they were never intended to be permanent memorials. Hatchments originated in the seventeenth century, although most surviving examples belong to the eighteenth and early nineteenth centuries. It is the treatment of the background that makes hatchments interesting – painting of the coat of arms is not always especially skilful or accurate. One side of the background was painted black to indicate the deceased, with the plain background indicating the surviving spouse. Fully black backgrounds were reserved for spinsters, bachelors and widows, with further variations for those with more than one spouse. Hatchments can be found in family chapels, or else high on the nave walls. St Mary and St Chad churches in Shrewsbury (Shropshire) have large collections, as does Stanford-on-Avon (Northamptonshire) (*colour plate 23*).

9

THE CHURCHYARD

CHURCHYARDS

The shape of a churchyard can reveal something about the history of a church. Circular churchyards are a sign of ancient foundation and Wales has many of them. In their present form, however, the churchyard walls are usually much later and belong to the post-Reformation period. Some even incorporate structures associated with rural life. Norton-sub-Hamdon (Somerset) incorporates a dovecote; Pembrey (Carmarthenshire), Penderyn (Glamorgan) and other rural churches of south-west Wales incorporate *ffalds*, or penfolds, where stray animals were kept until claimed by their owners.

The churchyard was a social venue in the medieval and later periods, used for outdoor social gatherings such as church ales that raised money to maintain and enhance the church. In the early medieval period business and other daily transactions took place inside the church. By the late medieval period some parishes had constructed separate church houses, the forerunner of the church hall, to conduct their secular business. Crowcombe (Somerset) church house was built in 1515 and continues to be used for its original purpose (*122*). Another well-preserved example is at Baltonsborough (Somerset), which is also still a parish room.

The main entrance to the churchyard is often through a lych gate, a covered gateway. Funeral rites of the Church of England began at the entrance to the churchyard, which encouraged the building of covered shelters over the corpse table upon which the coffin was laid. There are some surviving medieval examples – as at Whitbourne (Herefordshire), and Anstey (Hertfordshire) – but most date from after the Reformation. Many were built as late as the nineteenth century as part of the restoration of the church. The style of pre-

Victorian lych gates owes more to regional vernacular traditions than to the architecture of the church. Painswick (Gloucestershire) is an ambitious timber-framed building with a parish room above it; Llangelynin (Gwynedd) a more rugged and simple stone structure under a traditional stone-tile roof. Inside are wooden or iron gates, stone benches at the sides and, occasionally, a corpse table in the centre. Victorian architects included lych gates with the overall design of rural churches (and often rectories and church halls as well), making the lych gate and churchyard walls an integral component of the setting of the church.

Urban churches often have iron gates. Although most are nineteenth century and not especially notable, some are earlier and are worth visiting in their own right. The early eighteenth century was the peak of architectural ironwork, some of which was created in the form of churchyard gates. Robert Davies (1675-1748) of Croes Foel (Wrexham) is outstanding in this respect. His ecclesiastical commissions included churchyard gates at Ruthin (Denbighshire) dated 1728, Wrexham St Giles, Malpas (Cheshire) dated 1724 and Oswestry (Shropshire). In the south-west William Edney enjoyed a similar regional reputation and made the iron gates for Tewkesbury Abbey (Gloucestershire), a parish church since the Reformation.

MEDIEVAL CHURCHYARD CROSSES

Medieval crosses were common in parochial churchyards. They served as a universal grave memorial, and had a liturgical function as the second of the Stations of the Cross in the Palm Sunday procession, and where the Mass was celebrated. Churchyard crosses were traditionally an assembly point where churchwardens made various announcements. They also provided a platform for open-air preachers, origin of the term 'preaching cross'.

Typically they stand on a stepped plinth, have a square base turning to an octagonal tapering shaft. 'Cross' is a misleading term; in most cases they are crowned with a tabernacle carved with scenes such as the crucifixion, the rood (i.e. the crucifixion with Mary and John), and the Virgin and Child. Niches in each side were for the reserved sacrament from the Mass.

Opposite: 122 Crowcombe (Somerset) church house was built in 1515 and remains in use for its original purpose

Right: 123 Among the few surviving complete medieval churchyard crosses is this example at Trelawnyd (Flintshire)

The best-preserved churchyard crosses include the well-known example at Ampney Crucis (Gloucestershire) and the relatively unknown examples at Llangan (Glamorgan) and Trelawnyd (Flintshire) (*123*). Some have figures on the north and south faces, as at Hanmer (Flintshire), which has figures of St Chad and a mitred bishop. However, very few churchyard crosses have survived in their entirety. The tabernacles were an easy target for Puritan iconoclasts, or else their finely carved detail has slowly weathered over the centuries. In the nineteenth century some tabernacles were reinstated. Usually however, the churchyard cross survives only partially, either as just the plinth, or with all or part of the shaft. Plinths and shafts were ideal for converting to sundials in the eighteenth century.

MEDIEVAL CHURCHYARD MEMORIALS

Churchyards have always been used for burial. Early burials took place in the churchyard and within the church. Burial in the church, especially the chancel or near a side altar, was limited to priests and people of rank and wealth. Right to bury the dead in the churchyard was one of the distinguishing characteristics of the parish church, as opposed to the chapels of ease or early 'field churches' that were subordinate to them and did not have burial rights.

To reach the temple of life worshippers walk through the garden of death. In modern society the dead are kept well away from the living. In the less-sanitised medieval society and well into the twentieth century the dead were a part of everyday life and reference to them is the most conspicuous feature of most churchyards.

Early medieval commemorative stones are found mostly in Celtic Britain and the north of England. They vary in style but their function was similar, to commemorate illustrious and high-ranking people. The tendency to move old stones, whether for convenience or out of antiquarian interest, has meant these stones no longer stand over the graves of those they commemorate. They can be found in the churchyard or, especially if they are of antiquarian interest, inside the church. However, churchyard excavations have revealed the practice of erecting upright grave markers in the early medieval period, in some cases re-using earlier stones. Excavation at York Minster, for example, yielded a Roman inscribed stone re-used as a grave marker with the added inscription 'pray for the soul of Costavn'. Other excavated stones at York have retained fragments of pigment, showing that the stones were once painted. Excavation in the graveyard of Lincoln St Mark has revealed the base of a decorated upright stone laid directly above the chest of the deceased.

Among the earliest surviving upright memorials used for Christian burial are inscribed stones that bear no Christian iconography. Some of them, like the stones at Lewannick, Cardinham, St Clement and St Kew (all in Cornwall), have Ogham script of the sixth/seventh century. The densest concentration of Ogham stones in Wales is in Pembrokeshire, among which the stones at Bridell, Clydey and Maenclochog (taken from the lost church of Llandeilo Llwydiarth) all have crosses carved on them – although whether these were intended for Christian burial in the first instance, or whether they were subsequently re-used for Christian burial is an open question.

Other early Christian stones are the small worked stones carved with simple crosses, or the Chi-Rho monogram. They are numerous in Cornwall. Chi-Rho (written 'XP') refers to the first two letters of Christ's name in Greek. The monogram was popularised in the fourth century by the Roman emperor Constantine and was a common early Christian symbol. Good examples of these simple stones are at St Just-in-Penwith.

More elaborate sculpted crosses were carved from the ninth to the eleventh centuries (see 10). Nevern (Pembrokeshire) retains a high cross in the churchyard of the mid-eleventh century, as well as a fifth-century inscribed stone with Ogham script. Llandough and Llangan (Glamorgan) have early crosses in the churchyard. Cornwall has simpler crosses, including those of Cardinham and the 5.3m high cross at Mylor, although not every example of this type of cross is found in a churchyard. Celtic crosses are different in character from the early Christian stones in the north of England, but all served a similar purpose. Bewcastle, Gosforth (Cumbria), Corbridge and Rothbury (Northumberland) all have fine examples (124). Irton (Lancashire) is the sole example of this type that retains its cross head. Some exhibit Viking influence, like the cross shaft now inside the church at Nunburnholme (East Riding). Proliferation of crosses in the north of England, extending as far south as Lincolnshire and Derbyshire may well also have served to establish lordship. Some stones, such as the cross inside the church at Middleton (North Yorkshire), show warrior imagery.

124 The seventh-century cross at Bewcastle (Cumbria) retains its shaft but has lost its cross head. The shaft has exceptionally well-preserved carving, mainly of foliage. Who the cross commemorates is not known

Pressure on space led to the disturbance of burials to make way for a larger building or new interments. Early gravestones have been found during excavations and restorers have found gravestones built into the church walls, allowing them to be assembled and displayed for the modern visitor. The porch at Bakewell (Derbyshire) has a large collection of memorial stones from the tenth to the thirteenth centuries, discovered and assembled when the church was restored in 1841. Norman memorials decorated with elaborate knotwork and even figurative sculpture have survived inside a small number of parish churches, like the ornate examples at Northampton St Peter, Lewes (Sussex) and Conisborough (North Yorkshire). Gothic grave slabs are mostly crosses embellished with scrollwork or foliage. They can be seen in several places, like Kirkdale and Dewsbury (West Yorkshire). Medieval chest tombs survive in a small number of churchyards, the earliest probably that at Loversall (South Yorkshire), decorated with blind intersecting tracery and probably of the fourteenth century.

When graveyards had filled up the bones of earlier burials were removed to make way for the new, and were stored in charnel houses or ossuaries. Many of these were housed in crypts. Hythe (Kent) is the best known, where disarticulated bones are stored neatly on shelves in the crypt. Carew Cheriton (Pembrokeshire) has a fourteenth-century charnel house in the churchyard, which owes its survival to its conversion to a school room in the seventeenth century. It has a chapel, below which the ossuary is a barrel-vaulted undercroft with bone holes.

POST-REFORMATION CHURCHYARD MEMORIALS

Churchyard memorials became fashionable from the end of the seventeenth century. Use of local material has given many of these graveyards a distinctive character, like the Delabole slate of Cornwall, Caernarfonshire slate of North Wales, limestone monuments in the Cotswolds, and even some cast-iron headstones, like those of the Weald, close to the centre of the early iron industry. Headstones incorporate simplified forms of classical ornament familiar from tombs inside the church. They frame inscriptions, the earlier of which are sometimes in Latin. More ambitious memorials included various forms of chest tombs and table tombs – where a grave slab was raised up at the corners on moulded stone legs. Other forms of monument gained ground from the end of the eighteenth century, including pedestals and obelisks. The Gothic revival brought new motifs to established forms such as tomb chests and obelisks, and tombs in imitation of medieval shrines. The nineteenth century also saw standardisation of designs, encouraged by pattern books such as *Designs for Christian Memorials* (1868) by John Gibbs, and *Original Designs for Christian Memorials* (1864) by Theophilus Smith. Cast-iron railings were popular in the nineteenth century when they could be produced cheaply to standard patterns. Such railings afforded a degree of privacy for family tombs, and introduced the notion of private space. Towards the end of the nineteenth century came a Celtic revival, with early medieval Celtic crosses appearing as graveyard memorials (although the form found greater favour for public war memorials), principally in Cornwall and Wales.

WAR MEMORIALS

War memorials were often placed in churchyards where the church was the focal point of the community. Churchyard war memorials are therefore more common in rural than in urban churches. Designs varied greatly, but most comprise a tall stone on a plinth and base, either an obelisk, a crucifix or Celtic cross. Most of them are modest and it is difficult to single out individual examples. Hanmer (Flintshire) war memorial is a crucifixion in the style of a medieval churchyard cross, by Giles Gilbert Scott, with exquisite Arts-and-Crafts lettering on the base (*125*).

SUNDIALS

Churchyard sundials are a product of the post-Reformation period. As mentioned above, some were created by re-using the broken shaft of a churchyard cross. In other cases a stone pedestal, usually shaped like a wooden baluster, has a flat top on which the plate and gnomon were fixed. The metal plate bears the engraved dial, but it also often bears the names of the churchwardens and the maker, and many also supply the date. Gwaunysgor (Flintshire) has a sundial dated 1663, one of the earliest of the type. Neighbouring Cheshire also has many churchyard

125 The memorial to the 1914–8 war in the churchyard at Hanmer (Flintshire) is by
Giles Gilbert Scott and is closely modelled on a medieval churchyard cross

sundials, as at Alderly, Prestbury and Tilston. Conwy (Gwynedd) has a sundial dated 1761 and made by Meredith Hughes, at the expense of the Corporation.

YEW TREES

The yew tree is one of the longest-living native tree species, but not all churchyard yews are ancient. Many were planted in the nineteenth century, in the wake of J.C. Loudon's *On the Laying Out, Planting and Managing of Cemeteries* (1843). The yew is a manageable as well as a symbolic tree – apart from the association of evergreens with eternal life, yews do not drown gravestones in leaves every autumn. Historians have placed too much emphasis in trying to prove the longevity of yews, on the basis that the older a tree is the more valuable it becomes. Nevertheless some churchyards yews are undoubtedly ancient, although whether they pre-date the churchyards in which they stand is an open question. It is most likely that ancient churchyard yews were planted. There is evidence for the direct association of yews and early churches, but it comes mostly from Ireland rather than Britain. For example, a ninth-century poem refers to 'a tall bright glistening yew' behind the sanctuary of the Columban monastery of Durrow, suggesting that Mass was celebrated close to or beneath a yew tree that pre-dated Christianity. In medieval Britain fronds of yew (and willow and box), blessed with incense and holy water, were used in Palm Sunday processions in place of palms. Known as the 'hallowing of fronds', it existed from at least the eighth century.

The oldest churchyard yews have probably lived for more than a thousand years. However, precise dating is not possible because the core of the trunk rots away, leaving hollow living trees without their earliest growth rings. There are only a small number of these trees, and they have long been celebrated. John Evelyn remarked upon the antiquity of the Crowhurst (Surrey) yew in the 1660s. In 1662 Totteridge (Hertfordshire) yew had a girth of 9m, Llanerfyl (Powys) yew a girth of 12.2m. Other venerable churchyard yews are found at Much Marcle (Herefordshire) and Clun (Shropshire). At Rhulen (Powys) the stump of a former yew is directly outside the east end of the church and is the reason why the church has no east window.

FURTHER READING

There is an enormous number of publications on parish churches, but scholarship continues to enlarge our understanding of the subject and new perspectives are always welcome. However, many earlier books remain essential reading matter. The list below is a small selection of the most useful books, although not all are still in print. The best and most authoritative gazetteers are to be found in the volumes of the Buildings of England, Wales and Scotland by various authors. Individual topics related to parish churches are covered in many short publications by Shire. Church guide books are notoriously hit and miss but I can't remember one that was not worth buying.

Anderson, M.D., *History and Imagery in British Churches* (London, John Murray, 1971).

Burgess, Frederick, *English Churchyard Memorials* (London, Lutterworth Press, 1963).

Clifton-Taylor, Alec, *The Pattern of English Building* (London, Faber & Faber, 1972).
Clifton-Taylor, Alec, *English Parish Churches as Works of Art* (Oxford, Oxford University Press, 1989).
Coldstream, Nicola, *The Decorated Style: Architecture and Ornament 1240-1360* (London, British Museum Press, 1994).
Colvin, Howard, *A Biographical Dictionary of British Architects, 1600-1840* (2nd ed. London, John Murray, 1978).
Crewe, Sarah, *Stained Glass in England 1180-1540* (London, RCHME, 1987).
Cunningham, Colin, *Stones of Witness: Church Architecture and Function* (Stroud, Sutton, 1999).
Curl, James Stevens, *Victorian Churches* (London, Batsford and English Heritage, 1995).

Duffy, Eamon, *The Stripping of the Altars: Traditional Religion in England 1400-1580* (London, Yale University Press, 1992).

Fernie, Eric, *The Architecture of Norman England* (Oxford, Oxford University Press, 2000).
Friar, Stephen, *A Companion to the English Parish Church* (Stroud, Sutton, 1996).

Hadley, D.M., *Death in Medieval England* (Stroud, Tempus, 1998).
Harrison, Martin, *Victorian Stained Glass* (London, Barrie & Jenkins, 1980).
Harvey, John, *The Perpendicular Style, 1330-1485* (London, Batsford, 1978).

Harvey, John, *English Medieval Architects: A Biographical Dictionary down to 1540* (Stroud, Alan Sutton, 1984).
Howell, Peter, and Ian Sutton (eds), *The Faber Guide to Victorian Churches* (London, Faber & Faber, 1989).

Jeffrey, Paul, *The City Churches of Sir Christopher Wren* (London, Hambledon, 1996).
Jeffrey, Paul, *The Collegiate Churches of England and Wales* (London, Robert Hale, 2004).
Jenkins, Simon, *England's Thousand Best Churches* (London, Penguin, 2000).

Lees, Hilary, *Exploring English Churchyard Memorials* (Stroud, Tempus, 2002).

Marks, Richard, *Stained Glass in England during the Middle Ages* (London, Routledge, 1993).
Morris, Richard, *Churches in the Landscape* (London, Dent, 1989).

NADFAS, *Inside Churches: A guide to church furnishing* (London, Capability Publishing, revised ed. 1993).

Osborne, June, *Stained Glass in England* (Stroud, Sutton, 1997).

Platt, Colin, *The Parish Churches of Medieval England* (London, Secker & Warburg, 1981).
Port, M.H., *Six Hundred New Churches: A study of the Church Building Commission 1818-56* (London, SPCK, 1961).

Rodwell, Warwick, *The Archaeology of Churches* (Stroud, Tempus, 2005).

Stamp, Gavin, *The Twentieth-Century Church* (London, the Twentieth-Century Society, 1998).

Taylor, Richard, *How to read a Church: A guide to images, symbols and meanings in churches and cathedrals* (London, Rider & Co., 2003).
Thurlby, Malcolm, *The Herefordshire School of Romanesque Sculpture* (Almeley, Logaston Press, 1999).

Yates, Nigel, *Buildings, Faith and Worship: the liturgical arrangement of Anglican churches* (Oxford, Oxford University Press, 1991).

INDEX OF CHURCHES
BY PLACE NAME

GENERAL INDEX